NINJA LUXE CAF
COOKBOOK FOR BEGINNERS

300 Barista Recipes for Bold Espressos, Luxe Lattes & Seasonal Sips

ANNABEL HARTLEY

A Special Thank You

I would like to take a moment to express my sincere gratitude from the bottom of my heart for choosing this book. By picking up *Ninja Luxe Café Cookbook for Beginners*, you're unlocking a world of delicious coffee experiences right in your own home. Whether you're brewing your first espresso shot or perfecting your signature latte, this book is here to help you make every sip something special.

This book was created with you in mind: your passion for coffee, your love for trying new flavors, and your desire to elevate your café experience at home. Every recipe, tip, and technique was carefully crafted to ensure that your Ninja Luxe Café machine becomes a trusted companion in your journey to great coffee.

Thank you for allowing me to be a part of your journey. I'm excited to see the creative drinks you'll brew, and I hope this book brings joy, comfort, and a bit of café magic into your daily routine.

With warmth and gratitude,
ANNABEL HARTLEY

TABLE OF CONTENTS

INTRODUCTION

Imagine this: it's a chilly morning, the kind where even the thought of stepping outside feels heavy. You walk into your kitchen, still wrapped in the quiet of the early hours. Instead of rushing to a crowded café or fumbling with a complicated machine, you press a button. Within moments, the rich aroma of freshly brewed espresso fills the air, warm milk froths to silky perfection, and you cradle a cup that tastes just as good, if not better than what you would have ordered from a barista. That is the everyday magic of the Ninja Luxe Café.

Owning a Ninja Luxe Café Premier or Pro Series is more than just buying another appliance. It's choosing convenience, creativity, and comfort all in one. For beginners, especially, this machine takes away the guesswork and turns what could be intimidating into something joyful.

The Heart of Café Culture

For me, coffee has always been more than a drink; it's a moment. I remember the mornings when the aroma of fresh espresso filled the air, wrapping me in comfort before the day even began. I've sat by café windows on rainy afternoons, watching the world pass by with a warm latte in my hands, and I've shared laughter with friends over cups of foamy cappuccinos. These small rituals are what make café culture special. It's about slowing down, savoring flavors, and creating memories around the table.

When I set out to write this cookbook, I didn't just want to share recipes. I tried to capture that feeling, the coziness of a café corner, the excitement of discovering a new flavor, and the warmth of connection that coffee brings.

Every recipe here is a piece of that experience, meant to bring café magic into your home.

So as you turn the pages, I invite you to not only try the drinks but also create your own rituals. Light a candle, play soft music, or share a cup with someone you love. Let these recipes be more than instructions; let them become part of your story.

Four Machines in One

Most machines specialize in one thing. Some handle espresso, others only make drip coffee. The Ninja Luxe Café does it all:

- **Espresso brewing** for classic shots, whether single, double, quad, ristretto, or lungo.

- **Drip coffee styles** that range from classic to rich, or even over ice, in multiple cup sizes.

- **Cold brew functions** that create smooth, refreshing drinks without hours of waiting.

- **An independent hot water system** so you can prepare tea, hot chocolate, or Americanos with ease.

This versatility means no cluttered countertops, no juggling multiple gadgets. Whether it's your wake-up espresso, an iced drink for a hot afternoon, or a cozy evening tea, your machine adapts to your needs.

Made for Beginners, Loved by All

Many new coffee drinkers feel nervous: "What if I grind it wrong? What if it's too bitter?" The Ninja Luxe Café answers those worries with smart features like **Barista**

Assist Technology. This system recommends grind sizes, adjusts brewing pressure and temperature, and ensures every cup is balanced.

It feels like having a patient barista standing beside you, guiding you step by step. Even if you've never pulled a shot before, you'll get results that make you smile.

Endless Variety Without Intimidation

Think about your favorite café menu. One day you crave a simple cappuccino, another day something seasonal like a pumpkin latte, and on weekends maybe a caramel cold brew. With the Ninja Luxe Café, that menu lives in your kitchen. From frothed milk to cold foam to syrups, it encourages you to explore without fear.

And because it grows with you, beginners become confident, and confident home brewers become creators.

Confidence in Every Cup

Every part of this machine is designed to reduce mistakes. The **integrated grinder and tamper** ensure consistency. The **Dual Froth System Pro** lets you choose your foam style without fuss. Instead of trial and error, you get repeatable results, rich, flavorful drinks that become part of your routine.

An Everyday Upgrade

Coffee isn't just about caffeine; it's about how it makes you feel. That first sip in the morning sets the tone for the day. With this machine, your kitchen becomes a place of warmth and ritual. No long lines, no overpriced cups, no frustration, just the quiet joy of knowing you can create something special, anytime you want.

As the owner of the Ninja Luxe Café Premier or Pro Series, you've made more than a purchase — you've made a lifestyle choice. This machine isn't here to limit you; it's here to grow with you. From your first espresso shot to experimenting with seasonal specials, it gives you the tools, the guidance, and the freedom to become your own barista.

In short, the Ninja Luxe Café is a game-changer because it transforms ordinary moments into café-quality experiences one cup at a time.

How to Use This Book

This cookbook is designed to be simple, practical, and packed with value. It is written in **black and white**, with a focus on what matters most: recipes. By keeping the format clean, you can fit more recipes per page and create a book that feels like a true guide, rather than a magazine.

Whether you own the **Premier** or **Pro Series**, this book covers both. When steps differ slightly between models, you'll see clear notes. Recipes are written in **dual measurements** US (cups, ounces, Fahrenheit) and UK/metric (grams, milliliters, Celsius), so no matter where you live, you can follow along without confusion.

How Recipes Are Organized

Recipes are grouped by style, just like a café menu:

- **Espresso recipes** for strong, bold shots.

- **Lattes and cappuccinos** for creamy comfort.

- **Cold brews and iced coffees** for refreshing drinks.

- **Seasonal specials** for festive favorites.
- **Café desserts and treats** for indulgent moments.
- **Dairy-free and blended drinks** for modern twists.
- **Syrups and toppings** to customize your creations.

Each section offers dozens of recipes, giving you over **300 ways** to explore your Ninja Luxe Café. The abundance is intentional. The more options you have, the more value you get from your machine.

The Three Stages of Every Drink

To avoid bulky instructions later, this introduction teaches you the **three main stages** of using your Ninja Luxe Café. Every recipe builds on these steps:

1. Grinding

- Use the integrated grinder.
- Select a grind size: **fine** for espresso, **medium** for drip, **coarse** for cold brew.
- Lock the portafilter and tamp evenly with the built-in tamper.
- Tip: Too sour? Grind finer. Too bitter? Grind coarser.

2. Brewing

- Choose your mode: **espresso, drip, cold brew, or hot water.**
- Select your size (single, double, quad, or ounces for drip/cold brew).
- Press brew — the machine adjusts pressure and temperature automatically.

3. Frothing

- Use the Dual Froth System Pro.
- Select from: steamed milk, thin froth, thick froth, extra-thick froth, or cold foam.
- Works with dairy and plant-based milks.
- Tip: Cold foam is perfect for iced drinks; steamed milk makes silky lattes.

What This Means for You

Because these three stages are explained once here, recipes won't repeat bulky instructions. Instead, each recipe gives you short, direct steps like: *"Grind medium-fine, brew a double shot, top with thick froth."* You'll always know what to do because the foundation is right here.

A Cookbook Built for Daily Use

Use this book however you like: flip to seasonal specials when holidays approach, try a new latte every week, or experiment with toppings when guests visit. The goal is not just to follow recipes, but to feel confident enough to create your own variations.

You now have a guide that is **organized, abundant, and clear,** a true partner to your Ninja Luxe Café Premier or Pro. With every page, you'll be ready to make café style drinks at home without stress or guesswork.

Meet Your Machine

Your Ninja Luxe Café Premier or Pro Series may look sleek and compact, but inside it holds the power of a full café setup. To feel confident, it helps to know the parts of your machine and what each one does. Think of this section as a guided tour. Once you know your way around, every recipe will feel easier.

The Main Parts of Your Ninja Luxe Café

1. Portafilter

- The portafilter is the handle with a basket where you place ground coffee.

- It locks into the group head, creating a tight seal for espresso brewing.

- Use single, double, or luxe baskets depending on recipe size.

- This is the starting point of **grinding → Brewing** in your machine.

2. Integrated Grinder

- Built right into the machine, so no need for a separate grinder.

- Offers up to 25 grind settings, from fine (espresso) to coarse (cold brew).

- Delivers fresh grounds directly into the portafilter — less mess, more precision.

- Works with **Barista Assist Technology**, which recommends the grind size for each drink.

- After grinding, tamp with the built-in tamper for even extraction.

3. Dual Froth System Pro

- A steam wand with five presets: steamed milk, thin froth, thick froth, extra-thick froth, and cold foam.

- The XL milk jug lets you froth enough for two drinks at once.

- Foam consistency changes the drink's feel: silky microfoam for lattes, dense froth for cappuccinos, chilled foam for iced drinks.

- Suitable for dairy and plant-based milks.

- This is the heart of the **Frothing** stage.

4. Independent Hot Water System

- Works separately from coffee brewing.

- Dispenses hot water for Americanos, tea, instant soups, or hot chocolate.

- Means you can brew coffee while still having hot water ready for other uses.

- A small but powerful feature — no extra kettle needed.

5. Control Panel

- The "dashboard" where you choose grind, brew, and froth settings.

- Clear buttons guide you through:

  - ❖ Espresso modes: single, double, quad, ristretto, lungo.

  - ❖ Drip coffee styles: classic, rich, over ice.

  - ❖ Cold brew options: cold brew coffee or cold-pressed espresso.

  - ❖ Froth settings: hot or cold, thin or thick.

- Premier and Pro models share the same logic, though the Pro has more advanced customizations.

How These Parts Work Together

Every drink follows the same flow:

1. **Grinding** – Choose a grind, fill the portafilter, and tamp.

2. **Brewing** – Select mode and size on the control panel.

3. **Frothing** – Steam or foam milk if the recipe calls for it.

By understanding where each stage happens on your machine, you'll never feel lost. You'll know the grinder prepares your base, the portafilter holds it steady, the control panel makes it brew, and the frother finishes the drink with style.

Premier vs Pro: A Quick Note

- Both models include all the essentials listed here.

- The **Pro Series** offers slightly more advanced custom settings for grind size and froth texture, giving you extra control if you want to experiment.

- The **Premier** keeps things simpler, making it friendlier for first-time users.

Your Café at Home

Once you're familiar with these parts, you'll see your Ninja Luxe Café for what it really is: a complete café system tucked into one machine. Instead of several gadgets cluttering your counter, you have one elegant tool that grinds, brews, and froths on demand.

Knowing your machine is the first step in becoming your own barista, and now, you're ready.

Overview of Features & Brew Modes

The Ninja Luxe Café Premier and Pro are more than coffee machines; they are complete café systems in one box. To get the best out of them, it helps to understand their key features and how each brew mode works. This section gives you a clear overview, with examples of drinks you'll be able to create.

Key Features

1. Barista Assist Technology

- Adjusts temperature and pressure automatically during brewing.

- Gives **grind-size recommendations** so beginners know exactly what to use.

- Prevents sour (under-extracted) or bitter (over-extracted) coffee.

- Example drinks: a single espresso shot that tastes balanced, or a rich lungo that isn't watery.

2. Integrated Grinder

- Built-in grinder with 25 settings — from **fine** (espresso) to **coarse** (cold brew).

- Delivers grounds straight into the portafilter, reducing mess.

- Ensures every recipe starts with fresh coffee, not stale pre-ground.

- Example drinks: fine grind for a **ristretto**, medium grind for **drip coffee**, coarse grind for **cold brew**.

3. Integrated Tamper

- Located on the machine for mess-free tamping.

- With a single push, it compresses grounds evenly — no need to worry about overflowing or uneven tamping.

- Consistent tamping means consistent flavor.

- Example drinks: perfectly even espresso shots for **vanilla lattes** or **mochas**.

4. Dual Froth System Pro

- Five preset froth textures: **steamed milk, thin froth, thick froth, extra-thick froth, cold foam**.

- Works with both dairy and plant-based milks.

- Large jug allows frothing for two drinks at once.

- Example drinks: silky steamed milk for a **cappuccino**, cold foam for an **iced brown sugar espresso shake**.

5. Cold Press Function

- Brews espresso at lower temperature and pressure for a smoother, less acidic flavor.

- Great for chilled drinks and cocktails.

- Example drinks: **cold-pressed espresso martini, lavender honey cold brew**.

6. Independent Hot Water System

- Dispenses hot water without interrupting coffee brewing.

- Useful for Americanos, tea, hot chocolate, or even instant noodles.

- Example drinks: **Americano, peppermint tea**, or **classic hot cocoa**.

7. Built-in Storage

- A compartment that holds baskets, cleaning tools, and the water test kit.

- Keeps everything tidy and within reach, so you're not searching drawers mid-brew.

Brew Modes

Espresso Types

- **Single Shot:** Strong and focused, perfect for a quick pick-me-up.

- **Double Shot:** Richer and fuller — the base for most lattes and cappuccinos.

- **Quad Shot:** For bold drinks or sharing.

- **Ristretto:** Shorter pull, intense flavor — ideal for coffee purists.

- **Lungo:** Longer pull, smoother taste — great for sipping slowly.

Example recipes: Vanilla Latte (double shot), Salted Caramel Cortado (ristretto), Mocha Luxe (lungo).

Drip Coffee Styles

- **Classic:** Clean and balanced, like traditional filter coffee.

- **Rich:** Fuller body with stronger flavor.

- **Over Ice:** Brewed at a strength that won't taste watered down when poured over ice.

Example recipes: Morning Drip (classic), Maple Pecan Drip (rich), Iced Honey Oat Coffee (over ice).

Cold Brew Options

- **Cold Brew Coffee:** Smooth, low-acid brew, ready faster than traditional overnight methods.

- **Cold-Pressed Espresso:** Stronger than cold brew, but smoother than hot espresso. Perfect for iced drinks and cocktails.

Example recipes: Spiced Apple Pie Cold Brew, Espresso Martini, Tropical Mango Cold Brew.

Hot Water System

- A simple mode, but one you'll use often.

- Dispenses hot water instantly — no kettle required.

- Ideal for making Americanos, teas, or diluting concentrated espresso.

Example recipes: Americano, Peppermint Tea, Hot Chocolate.

Putting It All Together

Every feature and brew mode is designed to work as part of the **Grinding → Brewing → Frothing** flow you've already learned. Grind fresh beans, brew in your chosen style, and froth if needed. Once you're comfortable, you'll be able to match features and modes with recipes at a glance.

With these tools at your fingertips, the Ninja Luxe Café transforms your kitchen into a café — versatile enough for quick mornings, cozy evenings, and everything in between.

Accessories & Setup Guide.

Unboxing and First Steps

Before your first brew:

- Remove all packaging materials.

- Wash any removable parts (portafilter, baskets, milk jug) with warm soapy water. Rinse and dry.

- Wipe down the exterior with a soft, damp cloth.

- Run a quick rinse cycle with plain water (no coffee) to clear the system.

Now, let's look at each accessory.

The Portafilter

- The handle that holds the basket where your ground coffee goes.

- Locks into the group head with a simple twist — you'll hear a click when secure.

- Use it for all espresso and cold-pressed coffee recipes.

Setup Tip: Always ensure the portafilter is dry before adding coffee grounds. A wet surface can affect tamping and extraction.

Baskets (Single, Double, Luxe)

- **Single basket:** For one shot of espresso or lighter recipes.

- **Double basket:** For two shots — the standard for most lattes and cappuccinos.

- **Luxe basket:** Designed for richer extractions or when brewing larger, specialty drinks.

Setup Tip: Choose your basket, drop it into the portafilter, and make sure it sits flat. Swap baskets depending on recipe size.

XL Milk Jug

- Stainless steel jug for steaming and frothing milk.

- Large enough to prepare foam for two drinks at once.

- Markings inside help you fill to the right level for different froth settings.

Setup Tip: Always start with cold milk for best results, whether dairy or plant-based. Cold milk froths more evenly.

Cleaning Brush

- Small, firm brush included for keeping the grinder, portafilter edges, and brew head clean.

- Use after each day of brewing to remove leftover grounds.

Setup Tip: Store the brush in the built-in compartment so it doesn't get misplaced.

Cleaning Disc

- A small insert is used when running the cleaning cycle.

- Place it in the portafilter during descaling or deep-clean routines.

- Ensures water and descaling solution flow evenly through the system.

Descaling Kit

- Includes descaling powder or tablets, plus a hard-water test strip.

- Use the strip first to see how hard your tap water is. Harder water = more frequent descaling.

- Follow the machine's cleaning cycle instructions with the powder/tablets to prevent buildup.

Built-In Storage

- A compartment that holds baskets, a cleaning brush, a cleaning disc, and other small tools.

- Keeps everything in one place so you're never searching for parts.

Preparing for Your First Brew

Once accessories are washed and in place:

1. Insert the basket of your choice into the portafilter.

2. Lock the portafilter into the group head.

3. Fill the water reservoir with fresh cold water.

4. Place your cup or jug under the spout.

5. The machine is now ready for grinding, brewing, or frothing according to your chosen recipe.

Why These Accessories Matter

Each accessory has a role: the portafilter and baskets give you flexibility, the milk jug unlocks creamy drinks, and the cleaning tools keep your machine in top condition. Together, they make sure your Ninja Luxe Café delivers café-quality results without extra equipment.

Barista Basics for Beginners

Learning to make great coffee starts with a few simple principles. Think of this as your quick-start guide to becoming your own barista. With the Ninja Luxe Café Premier or

Pro, you already have the right machine; now you just need to understand the basics that turn beans into delicious drinks.

Choosing the Right Beans

Coffee beans are like the foundation of a house: everything else depends on their quality.

- **Freshness matters:** Always look for beans roasted within the last month. Stale beans lose flavor quickly.

- **Whole beans are best:** Grinding fresh in your Ninja's integrated grinder keeps aroma and flavor locked in until the last second.

- **Origin and flavor:** African beans often taste fruity, South American beans nutty and chocolatey, Asian beans earthy and bold. Experiment to find what matches your taste.

Understanding Roast Levels

Roast is simply how long the beans are heated. Each level creates a different flavor:

- **Light Roast:** Bright, tangy, sometimes floral. Great for drip or cold brew.

- **Medium Roast:** Balanced, smooth, often nutty or chocolaty. Perfect all-rounder for espresso or lattes.

- **Dark Roast:** Bold, smoky, and strong. Excellent for rich espressos and drinks with milk.

Tip: If you love café classics like a caramel latte, medium roast is your safest bet.

Grind Size Basics

Think of grind size like texture in cooking. If you cut vegetables too big or too small, the recipe changes. Coffee is the same:

- **Fine (like table salt):** For espresso shots. Extracts quickly under pressure.

- **Medium (like sand):** For drip coffee. Balanced flow, not too strong, not too weak.

- **Coarse (like breadcrumbs):** For cold brew. Allows long steeping without bitterness.

Pro Tip: Too sour? Grind finer. Too bitter? Grind coarser.

Avoiding Sour or Bitter Brews

- **Sour = under-extracted.** The coffee water passed through too quickly. Try grinding finer or brewing longer.

- **Bitter = over-extracted.** Coffee brewed too long or too fine. Adjust to a coarser grind.

- **Fresh beans, correct grind, and balanced roast** are the trio that keep your coffee tasting right.

Weight-Based Dosing: Your Secret Weapon

Most machines guess by time. The Ninja Luxe Café is smarter; it uses **weight-based dosing**. That means it measures the actual weight of coffee grounds, not just grinding for a set number of seconds.

Why it matters:

- Consistency. Every shot tastes the same, every day.

- Balance. No more "too much coffee" or "too little flavor."
- Beginner-friendly. You don't need scales or guesswork; the machine does it for you.

Think of it like baking with a scale instead of eyeballing flour. More accurate, more reliable.

Bringing It Together

Great coffee isn't complicated. With fresh beans, the right roast, correct grind size, and consistent dosing, you already have the essentials. Your Ninja Luxe Café takes care of the details, so you can focus on enjoying the results.

This is the heart of being a barista at home: understanding the basics, trusting your machine, and enjoying every sip.

Understanding Brew Modes & Drink Styles

Espresso Shots

Single Shot

- **Flavor:** Intense, sharp, concentrated.
- **When to Use:** Quick pick-me-up or recipes that need only a small amount of espresso flavor.
- **Recipes:** Espresso con Panna, Vanilla Bean Affogato.

Double Shot

- **Flavor:** Rich and balanced, fuller body than a single.
- **When to Use:** The foundation of most café drinks.

- **Recipes:** Caramel Latte, Mocha Luxe, Dirty Chai Latte.

Quad Shot

- **Flavor:** Bold, heavy, and highly caffeinated.
- **When to Use:** Strong morning fuel or for sharing in blended drinks.
- **Recipes:** Quad Iced Mocha, Energy Shake Lattes.

Ristretto

- **Flavor:** Shorter pull, very concentrated and sweet-intense.
- **When to Use:** When you want espresso flavor without bitterness.
- **Recipes:** Salted Caramel Cortado, Cardamom Espresso.

Lungo

- **Flavor:** Longer pull, smoother, more diluted but still flavorful.
- **When to Use:** For sipping slowly or when you want an espresso taste in a larger cup.
- **Recipes:** Mocha Madness, Vanilla Lungo Latte.

Drip Coffee Styles

- ❖ **Classic Drip**
  - **Flavor:** Balanced, clean, familiar.
  - **When to Use:** Daily morning coffee or a base for adding syrups.
  - **Recipes:** Maple Pecan Drip, Morning Drip Coffee.

- ❖ **Rich Drip**
  - **Flavor:** Fuller body, deeper taste than classic.
  - **When to Use:** For coffee drinkers who enjoy a stronger flavor.
  - **Recipes:** Cinnamon Roll Drip, Nutty Hazelnut Drip.

- ❖ **Over Ice**
  - **Flavor:** Strong enough to hold up against melting ice without tasting watered down.
  - **When to Use:** Summer afternoons or iced latte bases.
  - **Recipes:** Iced Honey Oat Coffee, Brown Sugar Iced Latte.

Cold Brew Options

- ❖ **Standard Cold Brew**
  - **Flavor:** Smooth, low acidity, refreshing.
  - **When to Use:** When you want mellow coffee that's easy to sip.
  - **Recipes:** Spiced Apple Pie Cold Brew, Vanilla Sweet Cream Cold Brew.

- ❖ **Cold-Pressed Espresso**
  - **Flavor:** Stronger than cold brew, less bitter than hot espresso.
  - **When to Use:** For iced coffee cocktails or drinks that need bold flavor without heat.

  - **Recipes:** Espresso Martini, Lavender Honey Cold Brew.

Hot Water System

- **Flavor:** Neutral — simply clean hot water.
- **When to Use:** For teas, hot chocolate, Americanos, or quick instant meals.
- **Recipes:** Classic Americano, Peppermint Tea, Hot Cocoa Espresso Twist.

Why This Matters

Each brew mode has its own character. Choosing the right one isn't about rules, but about matching mood and recipe:

- Short and strong for espresso lovers.
- Smooth and mellow for cold brew fans.
- Balanced and cozy for drip drinkers.
- Simple and versatile for hot water uses.

By understanding these modes, you'll move through the recipes with ease, confident that you know exactly what each style delivers.

Grinding, Tamping & Timing

Great coffee starts with how you prepare the grounds. The Ninja Luxe Café Premier & Pro make this easier with a built-in grinder and tamper, but understanding the basics will help you get the best results every time.

The 25 Grind Settings

Your machine's integrated grinder has **25 levels**, allowing you to fine-tune flavor:

- **Fine grind (like table salt):** Best for espresso shots — fast extraction, bold taste.

- **Medium grind (like sand):** Ideal for drip coffee — smooth and balanced.

- **Coarse grind (like breadcrumbs):** Perfect for cold brew — long steep without bitterness.

Tip: Start with the recommended setting from Barista Assist. Once you gain confidence, experiment by adjusting finer or coarser to match your taste.

How to Choose the Right Grind Size

- **Espresso recipes:** Use fine to medium-fine. Too coarse, and the shot tastes weak.

- **Drip recipes:** Use medium. Too fine and it clogs the filter, causing overflow.

- **Cold brew recipes:** Use coarse. Too fine and the brew will turn muddy and bitter.

Think of grind size like seasoning food, just the right amount brings out flavor, too much or too little throws it off.

The Integrated Tamper

After grinding, the coffee in the portafilter needs to be pressed down evenly.

- Place the portafilter under the tamper slot.

- Push the lever gently, the tamper compresses the grounds smoothly.

- Even tamping ensures water flows evenly through the coffee, extracting flavor instead of leaving weak or bitter spots.

Without tamping, water finds "channels" and rushes through, making the brew taste inconsistent.

Why Timing Matters

Extraction time, how long water passes through coffee, changes the flavor:

- **Too fast (under 20 seconds):** Sour, under-extracted, weak taste.

- **Just right (20–30 seconds for espresso):** Balanced, rich, smooth.

- **Too long (over 35 seconds):** Bitter, over-extracted, unpleasant aftertaste.

The Ninja Luxe Café adjusts pressure and temperature for you, but your grind size and tamping affect timing. The machine and you work as partners here.

Troubleshooting Common Problems

- **Brew tastes too sour:**

  o Grind finer.

  o Tamp a little firmer.

- **Brew tastes too bitter:**

  o Grind coarser.

  o Reduce tamping pressure slightly.

- **Weak or watery coffee:**

  o Check you used the right basket size.

  o Ensure you tamped evenly.

- **Overflowing grounds:**

  o Portafilter may be overfilled.

  o Use the right basket for your recipe size.

The Key Takeaway

Grinding, tamping, and timing may feel small, but they shape every cup. With your Ninja Luxe Café, the built-in tools do most of the hard work. Your role is simply to guide them — choosing the right grind, tamping with care, and paying attention to timing. Once you practice, these steps become second nature, and your drinks will consistently taste like they came from a café.

Frothing Techniques Made Easy

The Ninja Luxe Café Premier & Pro includes the **Dual Froth System Pro**, giving you café-style milk textures at the press of a button. Frothing may look intimidating, but once you understand the five settings and how different milks behave, you'll be able to create silky lattes, foamy cappuccinos, and creamy iced drinks with confidence.

The 5 Froth Functions

- **Steamed Milk:** Smooth and silky, perfect for lattes or flat whites where you want a creamy base without heavy foam.

- **Thin Froth:** Light layer of foam that gently sits on top of drinks. Works well for macchiatos or lighter cappuccinos.

- **Thick Froth:** Denser foam, ideal for traditional cappuccinos or drinks that need more body.

- **Extra-Thick Froth:** Heavy, cloud-like foam that holds shape. Great for decorative toppings, indulgent mochas, or dessert-style drinks.

- **Cold Foam:** Froth without heat, smooth, creamy topping for iced lattes and cold brews. Keeps drinks refreshing while adding texture.

Dairy vs Plant-Based Milk

- **Dairy Milk:**
  - Whole milk froths the best creamy, stable foam.
  - 2% milk makes lighter foam, good for balanced drinks.
  - Skim milk creates lots of foam but less creaminess.

- **Plant-Based Milk:**
  - **Oat milk:** Best all-rounder, creamy and stable.
  - **Almond milk:** Froths lightly, with a nutty flavor.
  - **Soy milk:** Froths thickly but can taste beany if overheated.
  - **Coconut milk:** Creamy but less stable foam, adds tropical flavor.

Tips for Café-Style Textures

- Always start with **cold milk** for the best frothing results.

- Fill the jug only to the marked line — too much milk prevents proper foam.

- Hold the jug at a slight angle to let milk swirl evenly.

- For latte art textures, use steamed milk or thin froth.

- For cappuccinos, switch to thick or extra-thick froth.

Avoiding Common Mistakes

- **Watery foam:** Milk too hot or jug overfilled.

- **Large bubbles:** Start with cold milk and avoid old or low-protein milk.

- **Foam collapsing quickly:** Use fresh milk and avoid shaking the jug after frothing.

- **Burnt taste:** Don't re-froth milk that's already been steamed once.

Key Takeaway

Frothing is what transforms coffee into a café drink. With the Dual Froth System Pro, you don't need barista skills; just pick the right setting, choose the right milk, and let the machine guide you. Practice a few times, and you'll discover how much texture changes the personality of your drinks.

Cleaning & Maintenance

Daily Cleaning

Do these quick steps after each use:

- **Frother:**
  - Run a short burst of steam or foam with clean water to clear milk residue.
  - Wipe the wand with a damp cloth.

- **Portafilter & Baskets:**
  - Knock out used grounds.
  - Rinse with warm water and let dry.

- **Milk Jug:**
  - Wash with warm soapy water.
  - Rinse and dry thoroughly before next use.

Safety Tip: Never leave milk or grounds sitting overnight. They harden and become harder to clean.

Weekly Routines

- **Grinder Care:**
  - Use the included brush to sweep away leftover grounds.
  - Avoid water — only dry cleaning for grinder parts.

- **Drip Tray & Water Reservoir:**
  - Empty and wash with warm soapy water.
  - Rinse well and dry before replacing.

- **Descaling (if water is hard):**
  - Use descaling solution or tablets with the cleaning disc in the portafilter.
  - Run a full cycle following the on-screen prompts.
  - Rinse thoroughly with clean water afterward.

Monthly Maintenance

- **Deep Cleaning Cycle:**
  - Insert the cleaning disc into the portafilter.
  - Add descaling solution to the water tank.
  - Run the "clean" program to flush the system.

- **Water Hardness Test:**
  - Use the strip provided in your kit.
  - Adjust descaling frequency based on results:
    - Soft water = descale every 3 months.
    - Hard water = descale monthly.
- **Check Gaskets & Seals:**
  - Wipe rubber seals on the portafilter and water tank.
  - Replace if cracked or worn.

Why It Matters

- Clean parts = fresher flavor, no sour or burnt aftertaste.
- Regular descaling prevents mineral buildup that can damage heating elements.
- Proper grinder care ensures consistent performance.
- A well-maintained machine lasts longer and keeps every recipe reliable.

Troubleshooting Common Issues

Common Problems & Fixes List

Issue	Likely Cause(s)	Solution(s)
1. Weak or Watery Espresso	- Grind too coarse - Not enough coffee (dose too small) - Brewing ratio off (too much water for the amount of coffee)	- Use finer grind (one or two settings finer) - Use a correct basket (double or luxe for larger dose) - Adjust size/strength settings to match dose - Use weight-based dosing as recipes teach you
2. Espresso Tastes Sour (Under-extracted)	- Grind too coarse - Too short extraction time - Temperature too low - Beans too light or old	- Grind finer - Allow more brew time - Check machine pre-heat; ensure brew head and portafilter are warmed - Use fresher or medium/dark roast beans
3. Espresso Tastes Bitter (Over-extracted)	- Grind too fine - Extraction too long - Too much tamping pressure or uneven tamp - Beans are very dark or oily	- Coarsen grind - Reduce extraction time or stop the shot earlier - Tamp gently & evenly - Use lighter roast or cleaner beans

Problem	Cause	Solution
4. Overflowing Grounds / Mess During Brewing	- Portafilter overfilled - Ground coffee is not level or tamped evenly - Wrong basket size used - Moist or oily beans clumping	- Use the proper dose and basket - Level the grounds first; tamp evenly - Use dry, fresh beans; clean grinder regularly
5. Frother Not Producing Foam Correctly	- Milk temperature too warm/cold - Wrong milk type/low protein plant milk - Jug overfilled - Steam wand not cleaned and purged	- Always start with cold milk - Choose milk with good frothing properties (e.g., whole, oat, or a specifically frothing plant-milk) - Do not overfill; leave room for expansion - Purge wand before & after use; clean regularly
6. Grinder Jam / "Add Beans" or Hopper Blockage	- Beans are too oily or moist - Burrs clogged - Using beans with foreign objects like small pebbles - Hopper not seated properly	- Clean burrs & hopper; use brush - Use fresh dry beans - Shake out foreign debris - Ensure hopper is locked in place - If the "Add Beans" error appears, try removing & reseating the hopper or curry out burrs carefully
7. No Espresso Flow (Shot doesn't start)	- Grind is too fine → choking - Portafilter not locked correctly - Machine stalled or needs purge - Strength setting or brew size mismatch	- Coarsen grind - Check the portafilter is locked in place - Run a purge/cleaning cycle - Reset settings or try a smaller size
8. Machine Not Powering On / Error Codes / Leaks	- Power supply issues - Loose wiring or internal failure - Water reservoir incorrectly seated - Seal or gasket damaged or misaligned	- Plug into a known good outlet - Turn off, unplug, wait, then try again - Check all parts replaced correctly (water tank, portafilter) - Examine seals; if damaged, contact Ninja support - For leaks, isolate where water comes from (reservoir, portafilter, steam wand) and tighten or replace the part

Relatable FAQs Users Often Ask

These are real questions people have posted. If you're thinking "That's me!", try these:

- **"Why is my espresso so bitter every time?"**

  Usually over-extraction: grind too fine, extraction too long, or tamp too tight. Try a coarser grind, gentler tamp, shorter extraction.

- **"Why does the machine say 'Add Beans' when there are beans in the hopper?"**

  Often caused by a blockage in the burrs or hopper sensor. Clean the top burr, remove any stuck beans. Reseat the hopper properly.

- **"Why is my Barista Assist recommendation always the same, even with new beans?"**

  Barista Assist is a guide; it sometimes doesn't adjust perfectly for every single bean. Once you know your taste, tweak the grind size or strength manually until it tastes right.

- **"Why is the froth thin or disappearing quickly?"**

  Likely milk issue (protein level, freshness), or wand/foam system needs cleaning/purging. Also, check that milk is cold and you're not overfilling the jug.

- **"Why does the shot taste sour with my new beans, but the old ones were fine?"**

  It could be a lighter roast or a different processing; try a fine grind or increase brew temperature. Roast profile changes flavor a lot.

Safety Tips When Troubleshooting

- Always unplug the machine before inspecting internal parts.

- Avoid using excessive force. Parts like baskets, valves, or seals are fragile.

- Use only recommended cleaning tools. Never use harsh chemicals inside brew or steam paths.

When to Contact Support

If, after applying these fixes, you still have recurring issues like wildly inconsistent brew ratios, power failures, or sensor errors, it's time to reach out to Ninja support. Many issues are fixable with a firmware update, replacement seal, or sometimes factory repair; don't struggle silently.

Making It Part of Your Daily Ritual

Morning: A Confident Start

Mornings often feel rushed, but with one button, you can prepare a smooth drip coffee or a creamy latte. Instead of a long café line, you'll have your favorite drink ready before your toast pops. This quiet ritual sets the tone for the day, energized, calm, and in control.

Afternoon: A Lift Without Leaving Home

When energy dips, use your machine for iced drinks or a quick blended treat. An iced honey oat coffee or a refreshing cold brew can replace an expensive café run. These small breaks are not just about caffeine; they're about recharging your mood.

Evening: Winding Down

Evenings call for comfort. Switch to the hot water system for peppermint tea, a soothing chamomile, or rich hot chocolate with extra froth. These moments bring relaxation and remind you that your machine isn't only about coffee, it's about well-being.

Building Your Café Rituals

- Save money: Skip daily take-out drinks by recreating them at home.

- Impress guests: Offer cappuccinos or cold brews that look and taste café-made.

- Bring joy: Turn brewing into a ritual, the sound of grinding beans, the aroma filling your kitchen, the comfort of a warm cup in your hands.

With a little practice, your Ninja Luxe Café becomes more than an appliance; it becomes part of your story, making each day smoother, warmer, and more enjoyable.

Ingredients & Conversions

Café-Style Pantry Essentials

Coffee & Bases

- **Espresso beans:** Medium to dark roasts with chocolate or nutty notes are ideal.

- **Drip beans:** Medium roast for balance, lighter roast if you like brighter flavors.

- **Cold brew beans:** Coarse ground, smooth, less acidic blends.

Syrups & Flavorings

- Vanilla, caramel, hazelnut, and mocha syrups.

- Seasonal flavors: pumpkin spice, gingerbread, peppermint.

- Honey, maple syrup, and agave for natural sweetness.

Powders & Mix-ins

- Unsweetened cocoa powder.

- Cinnamon, nutmeg, and cardamom.

- Matcha powder.

- Protein powders for smoothies and blended drinks.

Dairy & Non-Dairy Milks

- Whole milk for creamy lattes.

- Oat, almond, soy, or coconut milk for plant-based options.

Extras & Pairings

- Whipped cream, marshmallows, or chocolate shavings.

- Fresh herbs like mint or rosemary.

- Cheeses, pastries, or breads for café-style serving.

Ingredient Swaps: UK vs US Terms

- **Courgette (UK) = Zucchini (US)**

- **Aubergine (UK) = Eggplant (US)**

- **Coriander (UK) = Cilantro (US)**

- **Caster sugar (UK) = Superfine sugar (US)**

- **Icing sugar (UK) = Powdered sugar (US)**

- **Double cream (UK) = Heavy cream (US)**

This guide makes sure recipes feel natural no matter which side of the Atlantic you're on.

Conversions You'll Use Often

Temperature

- Celsius → Fahrenheit: $(°C × 9 ÷ 5) + 32$
- Fahrenheit → Celsius: $(°F − 32) × 5 ÷ 9$

Weights & Volumes

- 1 ounce (oz) ≈ 28 grams (g)
- 1 pound (lb) ≈ 454 grams (g)
- 1 cup ≈ 240 milliliters (ml)
- 1 tablespoon (tbsp) ≈ 15 ml
- 1 teaspoon (tsp) ≈ 5 ml

Quick Conversion Tables

Volume Equivalents (Liquid)

US Standard	Ounces	Metric (Approx.)
2 tbsp	1 fl oz	30 ml
¼ cup	2 fl oz	60 ml
½ cup	4 fl oz	120 ml
1 cup	8 fl oz	240 ml
2 cups (1 pint)	16 fl oz	480 ml
4 cups (1 quart)	32 fl oz	950 ml (approx. 1 L)

Volume Equivalents (Dry)

US Standard	Metric (Approx.)
¼ tsp	1.25 ml
½ tsp	2.5 ml
1 tsp	5 ml
1 tbsp	15 ml
⅓ cup	80 ml
½ cup	120 ml
1 cup	240 ml
2 cups (1 pint)	480 ml
4 cups (1 quart)	950 ml

Why Conversions Matter

This book provides both US and UK/metric measurements, but learning these quick swaps helps you follow any recipe confidently. With a stocked pantry, simple swaps, and these conversion tools, you'll feel prepared no matter where you are in the world.

What's Ahead in the Cookbook

Now that you've learned the basics, it's time to step into the heart of this book: the recipes. Inside, you'll find **over 300 café-style drinks**, carefully organized to make your journey simple and enjoyable.

Think of the chapters as a menu at your favorite coffee shop:

- **Espresso Recipes** — classic single shots, doubles, quads, ristretto, and lungo, plus creative twists like pistachio espresso cream and affogatos.

- **Lattes & Cappuccinos** — silky, foamy favorites with flavors ranging from vanilla and caramel to seasonal pumpkin spice or peppermint.

- **Cold Brews & Iced Coffees** — smooth, refreshing drinks for warm days, including cold-pressed espressos and inventive chilled blends.

- **Seasonal Favorites** — autumn maple lattes, winter mochas, spring bloom drinks, and summer coolers that match the rhythm of the year.

- **Café-Style Specials** — indulgent treats like tiramisu lattes, affogato sundaes, churro lattes, and mocha shakes.

- **Dairy-Free & Blended Beauties** — oat, almond, and coconut creations designed for today's plant-based coffee lovers.

- **Frozen & Blended Drinks** — smoothies, frappes, and creamy shakes for a fun twist.

- **Syrups, Toppings & Add-Ons** — the extras that make each cup unique, from vanilla bean syrup to cold foam and chocolate dusting.

Every recipe works with both the **Ninja Luxe Café Premier and Pro Series**. Where features differ, you'll find clear notes so no owner feels left out.

This book is presented in **black and white**, with a focus on **easy-to-follow instructions** instead of glossy photos. The advantage? More space for recipes — more value for you. Whether you're after a quick morning latte or an impressive drink for guests, you'll always find something fresh to try.

Your home café journey begins now. Turn the page, choose your first recipe, and discover just how much your Ninja Luxe Café can do.

ESPRESSO RECIPES

For all espresso recipes in this section, use a **fine grind** unless a recipe specifies otherwise.

Classic Single Espresso Shot

- Yield: 1 shot (1 oz / 30 ml)
- Brew Time: ~25 sec
- Froth Time: None

Ingredients

- 0.35 oz (10 g) espresso beans, medium to dark roast

Instructions

- Select **Espresso Mode → Single Shot**.
- Grind beans fine (like table salt).
- Fill the single basket, level, and tamp evenly.
- Lock the portafilter into place, place the cup under the spout, and press brew.

Premier vs Pro Note

- Pro allows slight temperature adjustment; Premier auto-balances.

Quick Tip/Variation

- Warm your cup with hot water first to keep the espresso hotter for longer.

Double Espresso Shot

- Yield: 2 shots (2 oz / 60 ml)
- Brew Time: ~30 sec
- Froth Time: None

Ingredients

- 0.7 oz (20 g) espresso beans, medium to dark roast

Instructions

- Select **Espresso Mode → Double Shot**.
- Grind beans fine and fill double basket.
- Tamp evenly and lock into place.
- Press brew and collect in a 2–3 oz cup.

Quick Tip/Variation

- The double shot is the **foundation** for most lattes and cappuccinos — master this first.

Quad Espresso Shot

- Yield: 4 shots (4 oz / 120 ml)
- Brew Time: ~45 sec
- Froth Time: None

Ingredients

- 1.4 oz (40 g) espresso beans, medium to dark roast

Instructions

- Select **Espresso Mode → Quad Shot**.
- Grind beans fine and load into the luxe basket.

- Tamp evenly and lock the portafilter.
- Brew and serve in a larger cup (6–8 oz).

Quick Tip/Variation

- Great for **iced espresso drinks** or energy blends — smooth but powerful.

Ristretto (Short, Intense Espresso)

- Yield: 1 short shot (0.75 oz / 22 ml)
- Brew Time: ~15–20 sec
- Froth Time: None

Ingredients

- 0.35 oz (10 g) espresso beans, medium roast

Instructions

- Select **Espresso Mode → Ristretto**.
- Grind extra fine (slightly finer than espresso).
- Tamp firmly and brew — shorter extraction will run naturally.

Quick Tip/Variation

- Sweeter and less bitter than espresso. Perfect for cortados or dessert drinks.

Lungo (Long, Smooth Espresso)

- Yield: 1 lungo (3 oz / 90 ml)
- Brew Time: ~35 sec
- Froth Time: None

Ingredients

- 0.5 oz (14 g) espresso beans, medium roast

Instructions

- Select **Espresso Mode → Lungo**.
- Grind fine (standard espresso size).
- Tamp lightly, lock the portafilter, and brew — the machine will use more water for a longer shot.

Quick Tip/Variation

- Excellent for sipping slowly or as a **base for mochas and lattes**.

Salted Caramel Cortado

- Yield: 1 cortado (3 oz / 90 ml)
- Brew Time: ~25 sec
- Froth Time: ~30 sec

Ingredients

- 0.35 oz (10 g) espresso beans
- 2 oz (60 ml) steamed milk
- 1 tsp caramel syrup
- Pinch of sea salt

Instructions

- Select **Espresso Mode → Ristretto**.
- Grind extra fine and tamp firmly.
- Brew 1 short shot into a small glass.
- Froth milk lightly (thin froth) and pour over espresso.
- Stir in caramel syrup and sprinkle with sea salt.

- Swap sea salt for smoked salt for a gourmet twist.

Vanilla Bean Affogato Shot

- Yield: 1 serving
- Brew Time: ~25 sec
- Froth Time: None

Ingredients

- 0.35 oz (10 g) espresso beans
- 1 scoop vanilla bean ice cream

Instructions

- Select **Espresso Mode → Single Shot**.
- Grind fine, tamp, and brew directly over ice cream in a small bowl.
- Serve immediately with a spoon.

Quick Tip/Variation

- Try hazelnut gelato instead of vanilla for a richer flavor.

Café Miel (Honey-Cinnamon Espresso)

- Yield: 1 cup (6 oz / 180 ml)
- Brew Time: ~25 sec
- Froth Time: ~45 sec

Ingredients

- 0.35 oz (10 g) espresso beans
- ½ cup (120 ml) milk
- 1 tbsp honey

- ¼ tsp ground cinnamon

Instructions

- Select **Espresso Mode → Single Shot**.
- Brew espresso into a mug.
- Froth milk to thin the froth texture.
- Stir honey and cinnamon into espresso, then add milk.

Quick Tip/Variation

- Sprinkle cinnamon on top for aroma and presentation.

Mocha Luxe (Espresso + Chocolate Elegance)

- Yield: 1 mocha (8 oz / 240 ml)
- Brew Time: ~30 sec
- Froth Time: ~45 sec

Ingredients

- 0.7 oz (20 g) espresso beans
- ¾ cup (180 ml) milk
- 2 tbsp cocoa powder or chocolate syrup
- Whipped cream (optional)

Instructions

- Select **Espresso Mode → Double Shot**.
- Brew espresso into a mug.
- Mix cocoa powder or syrup into the espresso until smooth.
- Froth milk to a steamed texture and pour over.

- Top with whipped cream if desired.

Quick Tip/Variation

- Add a dash of cinnamon for a spicy Mexican mocha style.

Coconut Espresso Cooler

- Yield: 1 glass (8 oz / 240 ml)
- Brew Time: ~30 sec
- Froth Time: None

Ingredients

- 0.7 oz (20 g) espresso beans
- ½ cup (120 ml) coconut milk
- ½ cup (120 ml) ice cubes
- 1 tsp sugar or sweetener (optional)

Instructions

- Select **Espresso Mode → Double Shot**.
- Brew espresso and let it cool slightly.
- Pour espresso over ice in a tall glass.
- Add chilled coconut milk and stir.
- Sweeten if desired.

Quick Tip/Variation

- Garnish with toasted coconut flakes for café flair.

Iced Brown Sugar Espresso Shake

- Yield: 1 glass (12 oz / 360 ml)
- Brew Time: ~30 sec
- Froth Time: None

Ingredients

- 0.7 oz (20 g) espresso beans
- ½ cup (120 ml) milk
- 2 tbsp brown sugar
- 1 cup ice cubes

Instructions

- Select **Espresso Mode → Double Shot**.
- Brew espresso and let it cool slightly.
- Blend espresso, milk, brown sugar, and ice until smooth.
- Pour into a tall glass and serve immediately.

Quick Tip/Variation

- Add a pinch of cinnamon for a warm spice note.

Pistachio Cream Espresso

- Yield: 1 cup (6 oz / 180 ml)
- Brew Time: ~25 sec
- Froth Time: ~45 sec

Ingredients

- 0.35 oz (10 g) espresso beans
- ½ cup (120 ml) milk
- 1 tbsp pistachio paste or finely ground pistachios
- 1 tsp sugar or honey

Instructions

- Select **Espresso Mode → Single Shot**.

- Brew espresso into a mug.

- Froth milk to a thick froth texture.

- Stir pistachio paste and sweetener into espresso, then add milk.

Quick Tip/Variation

- Garnish with crushed pistachios for added flavor and café-style look.

Espresso Martini (Alcohol Optional)

- Yield: 1 glass (6 oz / 180 ml)

- Brew Time: ~30 sec

- Froth Time: None

Ingredients

- 0.7 oz (20 g) espresso beans

- 1 oz (30 ml) vodka (optional)

- ½ oz (15 ml) coffee liqueur (optional)

- ½ oz (15 ml) simple syrup

- Ice cubes

Instructions

- Select **Espresso Mode → Double Shot**.

- Brew espresso and allow it to cool slightly.

- In a shaker, combine espresso, syrup, and ice (add vodka/liqueur if using).

- Shake vigorously and strain into a martini glass.

Quick Tip/Variation

- Omit alcohol and replace with 2 oz cold brew for a refreshing mocktail.

Pumpkin Spice Espresso Shot (Seasonal Favorite)

- Yield: 1 shot (1 oz / 30 ml)

- Brew Time: ~25 sec

- Froth Time: None

Ingredients

- 0.35 oz (10 g) espresso beans

- ½ tsp pumpkin spice syrup or puree

- Pinch of cinnamon

Instructions

- Select **Espresso Mode → Single Shot**.

- Brew espresso into a small cup.

- Stir in pumpkin spice syrup and cinnamon until smooth.

Quick Tip/Variation

- Top with whipped cream for a festive touch.

Peppermint Mocha Espresso (Holiday Favorite)

- Yield: 1 cup (6 oz / 180 ml)

- Brew Time: ~25 sec

- Froth Time: ~30 sec

Ingredients

- 0.35 oz (10 g) espresso beans

- ½ cup (120 ml) milk
- 1 tbsp cocoa powder or chocolate syrup
- ¼ tsp peppermint extract
- Whipped cream (optional)

Instructions

- Select **Espresso Mode** → **Single Shot**.
- Brew espresso into a mug.
- Stir cocoa and peppermint into espresso.
- Froth milk lightly and pour over.
- Garnish with whipped cream if desired.

Quick Tip/Variation

- Sprinkle crushed candy cane on top for a holiday café feel.

Gingerbread Spiced Espresso

- Yield: 1 shot (1 oz / 30 ml)
- Brew Time: ~25 sec
- Froth Time: None

Ingredients

- 0.35 oz (10 g) espresso beans
- ½ tsp gingerbread syrup or molasses
- Pinch of ground ginger, cinnamon, and nutmeg

Instructions

- Select **Espresso Mode** → **Single Shot**.
- Brew espresso into a cup.

- Stir in gingerbread syrup and spices until smooth.

Quick Tip/Variation

- Add a swirl of whipped cream for a festive café-style finish.

Maple Brown Sugar Espresso

- Yield: 1 shot (1 oz / 30 ml)
- Brew Time: ~25 sec
- Froth Time: None

Ingredients

- 0.35 oz (10 g) espresso beans
- 1 tsp maple syrup
- ½ tsp brown sugar

Instructions

- Select **Espresso Mode** → **Single Shot**.
- Brew espresso into a small cup.
- Stir in maple syrup and brown sugar until dissolved.

Quick Tip/Variation

- Sprinkle with a touch of cinnamon for warmth.

Hazelnut Truffle Espresso

- Yield: 1 shot (1 oz / 30 ml)
- Brew Time: ~25 sec
- Froth Time: None

Ingredients

- 0.35 oz (10 g) espresso beans

- 1 tsp hazelnut syrup
- 1 tsp chocolate syrup

Instructions

- Select **Espresso Mode → Single Shot**.
- Brew espresso into a cup.
- Stir in hazelnut and chocolate syrup until blended.

Quick Tip/Variation

- Garnish with grated chocolate for a truffle-like finish.

Almond Biscotti Espresso

- Yield: 1 shot (1 oz / 30 ml)
- Brew Time: ~25 sec
- Froth Time: None

Ingredients

- 0.35 oz (10 g) espresso beans
- 1 tsp almond extract
- ½ tsp sugar

Instructions

- Select **Espresso Mode → Single Shot**.
- Brew espresso into a cup.
- Stir in almond extract and sugar until smooth.

Quick Tip/Variation

- Serve alongside an almond biscotti for a perfect pairing.

Toasted Marshmallow Espresso

- Yield: 1 shot (1 oz / 30 ml)
- Brew Time: ~25 sec
- Froth Time: None

Ingredients

- 0.35 oz (10 g) espresso beans
- 1 tsp toasted marshmallow syrup
- Whipped cream (optional)

Instructions

- Select **Espresso Mode → Single Shot**.
- Brew espresso into a cup.
- Stir in toasted marshmallow syrup.
- Top with whipped cream if desired.

Quick Tip/Variation

- Torch mini marshmallows and float on top for café flair.

Caramelized Banana Espresso Shot

- Yield: 1 shot (1 oz / 30 ml)
- Brew Time: ~25 sec
- Froth Time: None

Ingredients

- 0.35 oz (10 g) espresso beans
- 1 tsp caramelized banana puree or syrup
- Pinch of cinnamon (optional)

Instructions

- Select **Espresso Mode → Single Shot**.
- Brew espresso into a small cup.
- Stir in caramelized banana puree or syrup.
- Sprinkle with cinnamon if desired.

Quick Tip/Variation

- Pair with a slice of banana bread for a café-inspired combo.

2Espresso con Panna (Whipped Cream Topped)

- Yield: 1 shot (1 oz / 30 ml)
- Brew Time: ~25 sec
- Froth Time: None

Ingredients

- 0.35 oz (10 g) espresso beans
- 1 tbsp whipped cream

Instructions

- Select **Espresso Mode → Single Shot**.
- Brew espresso into a demitasse cup.
- Top immediately with a swirl of whipped cream.

Quick Tip/Variation

- Dust with cocoa powder or cinnamon for extra flavor.

Espresso Romano (With Lemon Twist)

- Yield: 1 shot (1 oz / 30 ml)
- Brew Time: ~25 sec
- Froth Time: None

Ingredients

- 0.35 oz (10 g) espresso beans
- Lemon peel twist (about 2 inches)

Instructions

- Select **Espresso Mode → Single Shot**.
- Brew espresso into a cup.
- Rub lemon peel lightly along the rim of the cup, then drop it into the espresso.

Quick Tip/Variation

- Adds brightness to balance darker roasts — ideal for after meals.

Spanish Café Solo Espresso

- Yield: 1 shot (1 oz / 30 ml)
- Brew Time: ~25 sec
- Froth Time: None

Ingredients

- 0.35 oz (10 g) espresso beans, dark roast

Instructions

- Select **Espresso Mode → Single Shot**.
- Brew espresso into a small cup.

- Serve plain, strong, and without milk.

Quick Tip/Variation

- Use a very dark roast for authentic Spanish café flavor.

Cuban Espresso Shot (Cafecito)

- Yield: 1 shot (1 oz / 30 ml)
- Brew Time: ~25 sec
- Froth Time: None

Ingredients

- 0.35 oz (10 g) espresso beans, dark roast
- 1 tsp granulated sugar

Instructions

- Select **Espresso Mode → Single Shot**.
- Brew espresso, adding a few drops of sugar to a cup.
- Whisk vigorously to form a creamy paste.
- Pour the rest of the espresso over the paste and stir well.

Quick Tip/Variation

- Traditionally enjoyed in small groups — serve alongside friends for the full Cuban experience.

Turkish-Style Sweet Espresso

- Yield: 1 shot (1 oz / 30 ml)
- Brew Time: ~25 sec
- Froth Time: None

Ingredients

- 0.35 oz (10 g) espresso beans, dark roast
- 1 tsp sugar
- Pinch of ground cardamom (optional)

Instructions

- Select **Espresso Mode → Single Shot**.
- Brew espresso directly into a cup.
- Stir in sugar until dissolved.
- Add cardamom for a traditional Turkish-inspired flavor.

Quick Tip/Variation

- Serve in a small demitasse cup for authenticity.

Italian Espresso Macchiato (Foam-Topped)

- Yield: 1 shot (1 oz / 30 ml)
- Brew Time: ~25 sec
- Froth Time: ~30 sec

Ingredients

- 0.35 oz (10 g) espresso beans
- 1–2 tbsp frothed milk (thin froth)

Instructions

- Select **Espresso Mode → Single Shot**.
- Brew espresso into a small cup.

- Froth a small amount of milk until airy.
- Place a dollop of froth on top of espresso.

Quick Tip/Variation

- "Macchiato" means *stained* — just a touch of foam is all you need.

Dirty Espresso Chai Shot

- Yield: 1 shot (3 oz / 90 ml)
- Brew Time: ~25 sec
- Froth Time: None

Ingredients

- 0.35 oz (10 g) espresso beans
- 2 oz (60 ml) prepared chai tea concentrate
- ½ tsp sugar or honey (optional)

Instructions

- Select **Espresso Mode → Single Shot**.
- Brew espresso into a small cup.
- Stir in warm chai concentrate and sweetener if desired.

Quick Tip/Variation

- Try it iced by pouring over ice cubes for a refreshing twist.

Cardamom Rose Espresso

- Yield: 1 shot (1 oz / 30 ml)
- Brew Time: ~25 sec
- Froth Time: None

Ingredients

- 0.35 oz (10 g) espresso beans
- Pinch of ground cardamom
- 2–3 drops rose water

Instructions

- Select **Espresso Mode → Single Shot**.
- Brew espresso into a cup.
- Stir in cardamom and rose water until well mixed.

Quick Tip/Variation

- Beautifully aromatic — best enjoyed after dinner.

Lavender Honey Espresso

- Yield: 1 shot (1 oz / 30 ml)
- Brew Time: ~25 sec
- Froth Time: None

Ingredients

- 0.35 oz (10 g) espresso beans
- 1 tsp honey
- 1–2 drops food-grade lavender extract or syrup

Instructions

- Select **Espresso Mode → Single Shot**.
- Brew espresso into a small cup.
- Stir in honey and lavender until smooth.

- Garnish with a tiny sprig of dried lavender for presentation.

Mocha Mint Espresso

- Yield: 1 shot (1 oz / 30 ml)
- Brew Time: ~25 sec
- Froth Time: None

Ingredients

- 0.35 oz (10 g) espresso beans
- 1 tsp chocolate syrup
- 1–2 drops peppermint extract

Instructions

- Select **Espresso Mode → Single Shot**.
- Brew espresso into a small cup.
- Stir in chocolate syrup and peppermint until smooth.

Quick Tip/Variation

- Top with whipped cream and chocolate shavings for a festive treat.

Espresso Tonic (Espresso + Sparkling)

- Yield: 1 glass (6–8 oz / 180–240 ml)
- Brew Time: ~25 sec
- Froth Time: None

Ingredients

- 0.35 oz (10 g) espresso beans
- ½ cup (120 ml) tonic water
- Ice cubes
- Lemon slice (optional)

Instructions

- Fill a glass with ice and pour tonic water.
- Select **Espresso Mode → Single Shot**.
- Brew espresso and pour gently over tonic water.
- Garnish with a lemon slice if desired.

Quick Tip/Variation

- For less bitterness, use sparkling water instead of tonic.

Cold-Pressed Espresso (Smooth Brew)

- Yield: 1 shot (1 oz / 30 ml)
- Brew Time: ~45 sec (lower temp)
- Froth Time: None

Ingredients

- 0.35 oz (10 g) espresso beans

Instructions

- Select **Cold Brew Mode → Cold-Pressed Espresso**.
- Grind beans fine and load into the portafilter.
- Brew at the preset lower temperature and pressure.

Quick Tip/Variation

- Ideal base for espresso martinis or smooth iced drinks.

Espresso con Chocolate (Chocolate Shavings)

- Yield: 1 shot (1 oz / 30 ml)
- Brew Time: ~25 sec
- Froth Time: None

Ingredients

- 0.35 oz (10 g) espresso beans
- 1 tsp grated dark chocolate

Instructions

- Select **Espresso Mode → Single Shot**.
- Brew espresso into a small cup.
- Stir in grated chocolate until melted.

Quick Tip/Variation

- Use milk chocolate for a sweeter version.

Espresso con Leche (Spanish Style)

- Yield: 1 cup (6 oz / 180 ml)
- Brew Time: ~25 sec
- Froth Time: ~30 sec

Ingredients

- 0.35 oz (10 g) espresso beans
- ½ cup (120 ml) steamed milk

Instructions

- Select **Espresso Mode → Single Shot**.
- Brew espresso into a mug.

- Froth milk to a light steamed texture and pour over espresso.

Quick Tip/Variation

- For authentic Spanish style, use equal parts espresso and milk.
- Yield: 1 shot (1 oz / 30 ml)
- Brew Time: ~25 sec

Espresso Shot

- Froth Time: None

Ingredients

- 0.35 oz (10 g) espresso beans
- 1 tsp Nutella (hazelnut spread)

Instructions

- Select **Espresso Mode → Single Shot**.
- Brew espresso into a small cup.
- Stir in Nutella until smooth and creamy.

Quick Tip/Variation

- Top with whipped cream and a drizzle of Nutella for indulgence.

Cinnamon Roll Espresso

- Yield: 1 shot (1 oz / 30 ml)
- Brew Time: ~25 sec
- Froth Time: ~30 sec

Ingredients

- 0.35 oz (10 g) espresso beans
- 1 tsp brown sugar
- ¼ tsp ground cinnamon

- 1 tbsp frothed milk (thin froth)

Instructions

- Select **Espresso Mode → Single Shot**.
- Brew espresso into a small cup.
- Stir in brown sugar and cinnamon.
- Add a dollop of milk froth on top.

Quick Tip/Variation

- Sprinkle cinnamon sugar over the froth for a pastry-like finish.

Cookies & Cream Espresso Shot

- Yield: 1 shot (1 oz / 30 ml)
- Brew Time: ~25 sec
- Froth Time: None

Ingredients

- 0.35 oz (10 g) espresso beans
- 1 tsp crushed chocolate sandwich cookies
- 1 tsp cream

Instructions

- Select **Espresso Mode → Single Shot**.
- Brew espresso into a cup.
- Stir in crushed cookies and cream until blended.

Quick Tip/Variation

- Top with cookie crumbles for texture and fun presentation.

Salted Toffee Espresso

- Yield: 1 shot (1 oz / 30 ml)
- Brew Time: ~25 sec
- Froth Time: None

Ingredients

- 0.35 oz (10 g) espresso beans
- 1 tsp toffee syrup
- Pinch of sea salt

Instructions

- Select **Espresso Mode → Single Shot**.
- Brew espresso into a cup.
- Stir in toffee syrup and sprinkle with salt.

Quick Tip/Variation

- Use smoked sea salt for a deeper, café-gourmet vibe.

Almond Joy-Inspired Espresso

- Yield: 1 shot (1 oz / 30 ml)
- Brew Time: ~25 sec
- Froth Time: None

Ingredients

- 0.35 oz (10 g) espresso beans
- ½ tsp coconut syrup
- ½ tsp chocolate syrup
- ¼ tsp almond extract

Instructions

- Select **Espresso Mode → Single Shot**.

- Brew espresso into a cup.
- Stir in coconut, chocolate syrup, and almond extract.

Quick Tip/Variation

- Garnish with shredded coconut for a candy-bar finish.

S'mores Espresso Shot

- Yield: 1 shot (1 oz / 30 ml)
- Brew Time: ~25 sec
- Froth Time: None

Ingredients

- 0.35 oz (10 g) espresso beans
- 1 tsp chocolate syrup
- 1 mini marshmallow (toasted, optional)
- 1 tsp crushed graham cracker

Instructions

- Select **Espresso Mode → Single Shot**.
- Brew espresso into a cup.
- Stir in chocolate syrup.
- Top with a toasted marshmallow and sprinkle graham cracker crumbs.

Quick Tip/Variation

- Add whipped cream for a true campfire-style espresso.

Spiced Maple Espresso

- Yield: 1 shot (1 oz / 30 ml)
- Brew Time: ~25 sec
- Froth Time: None

Ingredients

- 0.35 oz (10 g) espresso beans
- 1 tsp maple syrup
- Pinch of cinnamon and nutmeg

Instructions

- Select **Espresso Mode → Single Shot**.
- Brew espresso into a small cup.
- Stir in maple syrup and spices until smooth.

Quick Tip/Variation

- Use smoked cinnamon for a deeper, autumnal twist.

White Chocolate Raspberry Espresso

- Yield: 1 shot (1 oz / 30 ml)
- Brew Time: ~25 sec
- Froth Time: None

Ingredients

- 0.35 oz (10 g) espresso beans
- 1 tsp white chocolate syrup
- ½ tsp raspberry syrup

Instructions

- Select **Espresso Mode → Single Shot**.
- Brew espresso into a cup.
- Stir in white chocolate and raspberry syrups until blended.

Quick Tip/Variation

- Garnish with fresh raspberries for a café-style look.

Churro-Inspired Espresso

- Yield: 1 shot (1 oz / 30 ml)
- Brew Time: ~25 sec
- Froth Time: ~30 sec

Ingredients

- 0.35 oz (10 g) espresso beans
- ½ tsp brown sugar
- ¼ tsp cinnamon
- 1 tbsp frothed milk (thin froth)

Instructions

- Select **Espresso Mode → Single Shot**.
- Brew espresso into a small cup.
- Stir in brown sugar and cinnamon.
- Add a touch of frothed milk on top.

Quick Tip/Variation

- Rim the cup with cinnamon sugar for a churro-like presentation.

Espresso Brownie Bomb (Dessert-Style)

- Yield: 1 shot (1 oz / 30 ml)
- Brew Time: ~25 sec
- Froth Time: None

Ingredients

- 0.35 oz (10 g) espresso beans
- 1 tsp chocolate syrup
- 1 tsp crumbled brownie pieces

Instructions

- Select **Espresso Mode → Single Shot**.
- Brew espresso into a cup.
- Stir in chocolate syrup and brownie crumbles.

Quick Tip/Variation

- Top with whipped cream and extra brownie crumbs for indulgence.

Espresso Irish Cream (Alcohol Optional)

- Yield: 1 shot (1 oz / 30 ml)
- Brew Time: ~25 sec
- Froth Time: None

Ingredients

- 0.35 oz (10 g) espresso beans
- 1 tsp Irish cream syrup
- ½ oz (15 ml) Irish cream liqueur (optional)

Instructions

- Select **Espresso Mode → Single Shot**.
- Brew espresso into a cup.
- Stir in syrup (and liqueur if using).

Quick Tip/Variation

- Top with whipped cream and chocolate shavings for a dessert-style drink.

Apple Pie Spiced Espresso (Fall Favorite)

- Yield: 1 shot (1 oz / 30 ml)
- Brew Time: ~25 sec
- Froth Time: None

Ingredients

- 0.35 oz (10 g) espresso beans
- 1 tsp apple pie syrup or concentrate
- Pinch of cinnamon

Instructions

- Select **Espresso Mode** → **Single Shot**.
- Brew espresso into a cup.
- Stir in apple pie syrup and cinnamon.

Quick Tip/Variation

- Pair with a slice of apple tart for a cozy fall pairing.

Eggnog Espresso (Holiday Special)

- Yield: 1 shot (1 oz / 30 ml)
- Brew Time: ~25 sec
- Froth Time: ~30 sec

Ingredients

- 0.35 oz (10 g) espresso beans
- 2 tbsp eggnog (steamed)
- Pinch of nutmeg

Instructions

- Select **Espresso Mode** → **Single Shot**.
- Brew espresso into a cup.
- Froth eggnog lightly and pour over espresso.
- Sprinkle with nutmeg to finish.

Quick Tip/Variation

- For extra richness, add a splash of rum or brandy (optional).

Honey Lavender Espresso

- Yield: 1 shot (1 oz / 30 ml)
- Brew Time: ~25 sec
- Froth Time: None

Ingredients

- 0.35 oz (10 g) espresso beans
- 1 tsp honey
- 1–2 drops lavender extract or syrup

Instructions

- Select **Espresso Mode** → **Single Shot**.
- Brew espresso into a small cup.
- Stir in honey and lavender until smooth.

Quick Tip/Variation

- Serve with a sprig of lavender for aroma and presentation.

Black Forest Espresso Bomb

- Yield: 1 shot (1 oz / 30 ml)
- Brew Time: ~25 sec
- Froth Time: None

Ingredients

- 0.35 oz (10 g) espresso beans
- 1 tsp chocolate syrup
- ½ tsp cherry syrup or puree
- Whipped cream (optional)

Instructions

- Select **Espresso Mode → Single Shot**.
- Brew espresso into a cup.
- Stir in chocolate and cherry syrup.
- Top with whipped cream if desired.

Quick Tip/Variation

- Garnish with a maraschino cherry for the classic Black Forest vibe.

Your Café Notes

LATTES & CAPPUCCINOS

Classic Vanilla Latte

- Yield: 1 cup (8 oz / 240 ml)
- Brew Time: ~30 sec
- Froth Time: ~45 sec

Ingredients

- 0.7 oz (20 g) espresso beans (double shot)
- ¾ cup (180 ml) milk
- 1 tbsp vanilla syrup

Instructions

- Select **Espresso Mode → Double Shot**.
- Brew espresso into a mug.
- Froth milk to a smooth, steamed texture.
- Pour milk over espresso and stir in vanilla syrup.

Quick Tip/Variation

- Add a sprinkle of cinnamon on top for extra warmth.

Caramel Latte

- Yield: 1 cup (8 oz / 240 ml)
- Brew Time: ~30 sec
- Froth Time: ~45 s
- 0.7 oz (20 g) espresso beans (double shot)
- ¾ cup (180 ml) milk
- 1 tbsp caramel syrup
- Caramel drizzle (optional)

Instructions

- Select **Espresso Mode → Double Shot**.
- Brew espresso into a mug.
- Froth milk to a light steamed texture.
- Pour over espresso and stir in caramel syrup.
- Drizzle caramel on top if desired.

Quick Tip/Variation

- Try salted caramel syrup for a sweet-salty flavor.

Mocha Latte (Espresso + Chocolate)

- Yield: 1 cup (8 oz / 240 ml)
- Brew Time: ~30 sec
- Froth Time: ~45 sec

Ingredients

- 0.7 oz (20 g) espresso beans (double shot)
- ¾ cup (180 ml) milk
- 1 tbsp cocoa powder or chocolate syrup
- Whipped cream (optional)

Instructions

- Select **Espresso Mode → Double Shot**.

- Brew espresso into a mug.

- Stir in cocoa powder or syrup until smooth.

- Froth milk and pour over espresso-chocolate mixture.

- Top with whipped cream if desired.

Quick Tip/Variation

- Sprinkle with cocoa powder for a café-style finish.

Hazelnut Latte

- Yield: 1 cup (8 oz / 240 ml)

- Brew Time: ~30 sec

- Froth Time: ~45 sec

Ingredients

- 0.7 oz (20 g) espresso beans (double shot)

- ¾ cup (180 ml) milk

- 1 tbsp hazelnut syrup

Instructions

- Select **Espresso Mode → Double Shot**.

- Brew espresso into a mug.

- Froth milk until silky.

- Pour over espresso and stir in hazelnut syrup.

Quick Tip/Variation

- Add a drizzle of chocolate syrup for a Nutella-inspired twist.

Cinnamon Roll Latte

- Yield: 1 cup (8 oz / 240 ml)

- Brew Time: ~30 sec

- Froth Time: ~45 sec

Ingredients

- 0.7 oz (20 g) espresso beans (double shot)

- ¾ cup (180 ml) milk

- 1 tsp brown sugar

- ¼ tsp ground cinnamon

- Whipped cream (optional)

Instructions

- Select **Espresso Mode → Double Shot**.

- Brew espresso into a mug.

- Stir in brown sugar and cinnamon.

- Froth milk to a creamy texture and pour over.

- Top with whipped cream if desired.

Quick Tip/Variation

- Dust the top with cinnamon sugar for a true pastry-like finish.

Honey Lavender Latte

- Yield: 1 cup (8 oz / 240 ml)

- Brew Time: ~30 sec

- Froth Time: ~45 sec

Ingredients

- 0.7 oz (20 g) espresso beans (double shot)

- ¾ cup (180 ml) milk
- 1 tsp honey
- 2–3 drops lavender syrup or extract

Instructions

- Select **Espresso Mode** → **Double Shot**.
- Brew espresso into a mug.
- Froth milk until smooth and creamy.
- Stir honey and lavender into espresso, then top with milk.

Quick Tip/Variation

- Garnish with dried lavender for aroma and presentation.

Brown Sugar Shaken Latte

- Yield: 1 glass (12 oz / 360 ml)
- Brew Time: ~30 sec
- Froth Time: None

Ingredients

- 0.7 oz (20 g) espresso beans (double shot)
- 1 tbsp brown sugar
- ½ cup (120 ml) milk
- Ice cubes

Instructions

- Select **Espresso Mode** → **Double Shot**.
- Brew espresso and pour it into a shaker with brown sugar and ice.
- Shake vigorously until chilled and slightly frothy.

- Pour into a tall glass and top with milk.

Quick Tip/Variation

- Add a dash of cinnamon for extra warmth.

Pistachio Latte

- Yield: 1 cup (8 oz / 240 ml)
- Brew Time: ~30 sec
- Froth Time: ~45 sec

Ingredients

- 0.7 oz (20 g) espresso beans (double shot)
- ¾ cup (180 ml) milk
- 1 tbsp pistachio syrup or paste
- Crushed pistachios (optional garnish)

Instructions

- Select **Espresso Mode** → **Double Shot**.
- Brew espresso into a mug.
- Froth milk until silky and creamy.
- Stir pistachio syrup into espresso, then pour in milk.
- Garnish with crushed pistachios if desired.

Quick Tip/Variation

- Add a drizzle of white chocolate for extra indulgence.

White Chocolate Latte

- Yield: 1 cup (8 oz / 240 ml)

- Brew Time: ~30 sec

- Froth Time: ~45 sec

Ingredients

- 0.7 oz (20 g) espresso beans (double shot)

- ¾ cup (180 ml) milk

- 2 tbsp white chocolate chips or syrup

Instructions

- Select **Espresso Mode → Double Shot**.

- Brew espresso into a mug.

- Stir in white chocolate until melted.

- Froth milk until smooth and pour over espresso mixture.

Quick Tip/Variation

- Top with whipped cream and a sprinkle of white chocolate shavings.

Matcha Latte (Green Tea + Espresso)

- Yield: 1 cup (8 oz / 240 ml)

- Brew Time: ~30 sec

- Froth Time: ~45 sec

Ingredients

- 0.7 oz (20 g) espresso beans (double shot)

- ½ cup (120 ml) milk

- 1 tsp matcha powder

- 2 tbsp hot water

- 1 tsp honey or sugar (optional)

Instructions

- Whisk matcha powder with hot water until smooth.

- Select **Espresso Mode → Double Shot** and brew espresso.

- Froth milk to a creamy texture.

- In a mug, combine espresso, matcha, and sweetener.

- Pour in frothed milk and stir gently.

Quick Tip/Variation

- Try iced: pour everything over ice for a refreshing boost.

Turmeric Masala Latte ("Golden Latte")

- Yield: 1 cup (8 oz / 240 ml)

- Brew Time: ~30 sec

- Froth Time: ~45 sec

Ingredients

- 0.7 oz (20 g) espresso beans (double shot)

- ¾ cup (180 ml) milk

- ½ tsp ground turmeric

- Pinch of black pepper and cinnamon

- 1 tsp honey or maple syrup

Instructions

- Select **Espresso Mode → Double Shot** and brew into a mug.

- Froth milk with turmeric, pepper, and cinnamon mixed in.

- Pour spiced frothed milk over espresso.
- Stir in honey or maple syrup.

Quick Tip/Variation

- Use coconut milk for a richer, earthy flavor.

Dirty Chai Latte

- Yield: 1 cup (8 oz / 240 ml)
- Brew Time: ~30 sec
- Froth Time: ~45 sec

Ingredients

- 0.7 oz (20 g) espresso beans (double shot)
- ½ cup (120 ml) milk
- ½ cup (120 ml) chai tea concentrate
- 1 tsp sugar or honey (optional)

Instructions

- Select **Espresso Mode → Double Shot** and brew into a mug.
- Heat chai concentrate and combine with milk.
- Froth the mixture until creamy.
- Pour frothed chai-milk blend over espresso.

Quick Tip/Variation

- Try it iced by pouring over a tall glass of ice.

Gingerbread Latte (Seasonal)

- Yield: 1 cup (8 oz / 240 ml)
- Brew Time: ~30 sec
- Froth Time: ~45 sec

Ingredients

- 0.7 oz (20 g) espresso beans (double shot)
- ¾ cup (180 ml) milk
- 1 tbsp gingerbread syrup or molasses
- Pinch of cinnamon and nutmeg
- Whipped cream (optional)

Instructions

- Select **Espresso Mode → Double Shot** and brew into a mug.
- Stir in gingerbread syrup and spices.
- Froth milk until smooth and pour over espresso mixture.
- Top with whipped cream if desired.

Quick Tip/Variation

- Garnish with a mini gingerbread cookie for a festive touch.

Pumpkin Spice Latte (Seasonal Bestseller)

- Yield: 1 cup (8 oz / 240 ml)
- Brew Time: ~30 sec
- Froth Time: ~45 sec

Ingredients

- 0.7 oz (20 g) espresso beans (double shot)
- ¾ cup (180 ml) milk
- 1 tbsp pumpkin puree

- 1 tsp pumpkin spice blend

- 1 tsp sugar or maple syrup

- Whipped cream (optional)

Instructions

- Select **Espresso Mode** → **Double Shot** and brew into a mug.

- Stir pumpkin puree, spice blend, and sweetener into espresso.

- Froth milk to a creamy texture and pour over.

- Top with whipped cream if desired.

Quick Tip/Variation

- Sprinkle extra pumpkin spice on top for a café-style finish.

Eggnog Cappuccino (Holiday Favorite)

- Yield: 1 cup (6 oz / 180 ml)

- Brew Time: ~30 sec

- Froth Time: ~45 sec

Ingredients

- 0.7 oz (20 g) espresso beans (double shot)

- ½ cup (120 ml) eggnog

- Pinch of nutmeg

Instructions

- Select **Espresso Mode** → **Double Shot** and brew into a mug.

- Froth eggnog until light and airy.

- Pour over espresso to create a foamy cappuccino texture.

- Sprinkle nutmeg on top.

Quick Tip/Variation

- Add a splash of brandy for a traditional holiday twist.

Toasted Marshmallow Latte

- Yield: 1 cup (8 oz / 240 ml)

- Brew Time: ~30 sec

- Froth Time: ~45 sec

Ingredients

- 0.7 oz (20 g) espresso beans (double shot)

- ¾ cup (180 ml) milk

- 1 tbsp toasted marshmallow syrup

- Whipped cream (optional)

- Mini marshmallows (optional garnish)

Instructions

- Select **Espresso Mode** → **Double Shot** and brew into a mug.

- Stir in toasted marshmallow syrup.

- Froth milk until creamy and pour over espresso.

- Top with whipped cream and garnish with mini marshmallows if desired.

Quick Tip/Variation

- Lightly toast marshmallows with a kitchen torch for café flair.

Peppermint Mocha Latte

- Yield: 1 cup (8 oz / 240 ml)

- Brew Time: ~30 sec
- Froth Time: ~45 sec

Ingredients

- 0.7 oz (20 g) espresso beans (double shot)
- ¾ cup (180 ml) milk
- 1 tbsp chocolate syrup
- ¼ tsp peppermint extract
- Whipped cream (optional)

Instructions

- Select **Espresso Mode → Double Shot** and brew into a mug.
- Stir in chocolate syrup and peppermint extract.
- Froth milk to a creamy texture and pour over the espresso mixture.
- Top with whipped cream if desired.

Quick Tip/Variation

- Sprinkle crushed candy cane on top for a festive holiday finish.

Salted Caramel Latte

- Yield: 1 cup (8 oz / 240 ml)
- Brew Time: ~30 sec
- Froth Time: ~45 sec

Ingredients

- 0.7 oz (20 g) espresso beans (double shot)
- ¾ cup (180 ml) milk
- 1 tbsp caramel syrup

- Pinch of sea salt
- Caramel drizzle (optional)

Instructions

- Select **Espresso Mode → Double Shot** and brew into a mug.
- Stir in caramel syrup and sea salt.
- Froth milk until silky and pour over espresso mixture.
- Add caramel drizzle on top if desired.

Quick Tip/Variation

- Use smoked sea salt for a gourmet twist.

Maple Pecan Latte

- Yield: 1 cup (8 oz / 240 ml)
- Brew Time: ~30 sec
- Froth Time: ~45 sec

Ingredients

- 0.7 oz (20 g) espresso beans (double shot)
- ¾ cup (180 ml) milk
- 1 tbsp maple syrup
- ½ tsp pecan syrup or extract
- Crushed pecans (optional garnish)

Instructions

- Select **Espresso Mode → Double Shot** and brew into a mug.
- Stir in maple and pecan syrups.
- Froth milk to a creamy texture and pour over the espresso mixture.

- Garnish with crushed pecans if desired.

Quick Tip/Variation

- Add a drizzle of caramel for extra depth.

Almond Milk Latte (Dairy-Free Classic)

- Yield: 1 cup (8 oz / 240 ml)
- Brew Time: ~30 sec
- Froth Time: ~45 sec

Ingredients

- 0.7 oz (20 g) espresso beans (double shot)
- ¾ cup (180 ml) almond milk
- 1 tsp honey or agave (optional)

Instructions

- Select **Espresso Mode → Double Shot** and brew into a mug.
- Froth almond milk until lightly airy.
- Pour over espresso and sweeten if desired.

Quick Tip/Variation

- Use vanilla almond milk for added flavor.

Oat Milk Latte (Dairy-Free Favorite)

- Yield: 1 cup (8 oz / 240 ml)
- Brew Time: ~30 sec
- Froth Time: ~45 sec

Ingredients

- 0.7 oz (20 g) espresso beans (double shot)
- ¾ cup (180 ml) oat milk
- 1 tsp maple syrup (optional)

Instructions

- Select **Espresso Mode → Double Shot** and brew into a mug.
- Froth oat milk until creamy.
- Pour over espresso and sweeten with maple syrup if desired.

Quick Tip/Variation

- Barista-style oat milk froths better and gives a creamier texture.

Coconut Milk Latte

- Yield: 1 cup (8 oz / 240 ml)
- Brew Time: ~30 sec
- Froth Time: ~45 sec

Ingredients

- 0.7 oz (20 g) espresso beans (double shot)
- ¾ cup (180 ml) coconut milk
- 1 tsp honey or sugar (optional)

Instructions

- Select **Espresso Mode → Double Shot** and brew into a mug.
- Froth coconut milk lightly (it creates more foam than cream).

- Pour over espresso and stir in sweetener if desired.

Quick Tip/Variation

- Garnish with toasted coconut flakes for a tropical vibe.

Soy Flat White Latte

- Yield: 1 cup (6 oz / 180 ml)
- Brew Time: ~30 sec
- Froth Time: ~45 sec

Ingredients

- 0.7 oz (20 g) espresso beans (double shot)
- ½ cup (120 ml) soy milk

Instructions

- Select **Espresso Mode → Double Shot** and brew into a small cup.
- Froth soy milk to a very silky, microfoam texture.
- Pour over espresso for a smooth flat white.

Quick Tip/Variation

- Use unsweetened soy milk for balance, or sweetened for a creamier flavor.

Spanish Café Bombón Latte

- Yield: 1 cup (6 oz / 180 ml)
- Brew Time: ~30 sec
- Froth Time: None

Ingredients

- 0.7 oz (20 g) espresso beans (double shot)
- 2 tbsp sweetened condensed milk

Instructions

- Select **Espresso Mode → Double Shot** and brew into a glass.
- Spoon condensed milk into the bottom before brewing.
- Allow layers of condensed milk and espresso to remain visible for effect.

Quick Tip/Variation

- Stir before drinking for a sweet, rich blend.

Vietnamese Iced Latte

- Yield: 1 glass (10 oz / 300 ml)
- Brew Time: ~30 sec
- Froth Time: None

Ingredients

- 0.7 oz (20 g) espresso beans (double shot)
- 2 tbsp sweetened condensed milk
- ½ cup (120 ml) ice cubes

Instructions

- Select **Espresso Mode → Double Shot** and brew into a glass.
- Stir in condensed milk until fully blended.
- Add ice and serve chilled.

Quick Tip/Variation

- For extra strength, brew a quad shot instead of a double.

Italian Cappuccino (Classic)

- Yield: 1 cup (6 oz / 180 ml)
- Brew Time: ~30 sec
- Froth Time: ~45 sec

Ingredients

- 0.7 oz (20 g) espresso beans (double shot)
- ⅓ cup (80 ml) milk (steamed)
- ⅓ cup (80 ml) milk foam

Instructions

- Select **Espresso Mode → Double Shot** and brew into a cappuccino cup.
- Froth milk to create equal parts steamed milk and foam.
- Pour steamed milk over espresso, then top with foam.

Quick Tip/Variation

- Sprinkle cocoa powder on top for café authenticity.

Dry Cappuccino (More Foam)

- Yield: 1 cup (6 oz / 180 ml)
- Brew Time: ~30 sec
- Froth Time: ~50 sec

Ingredients

- 0.7 oz (20 g) espresso beans (double shot)

- ¼ cup (60 ml) steamed milk
- ½ cup (120 ml) thick milk foam

Instructions

- Select **Espresso Mode → Double Shot** and brew into a cup.
- Froth milk until airy and thick.
- Pour just a splash of steamed milk, then top with a large layer of foam.

Quick Tip/Variation

- Perfect for those who enjoy a lighter, airy texture.

Wet Cappuccino (Creamier)

- Yield: 1 cup (6 oz / 180 ml)
- Brew Time: ~30 sec
- Froth Time: ~40 sec

Ingredients

- 0.7 oz (20 g) espresso beans (double shot)
- ½ cup (120 ml) steamed milk
- ¼ cup (60 ml) light milk foam

Instructions

- Select **Espresso Mode → Double Shot** and brew into a mug.
- Froth milk lightly to create more steamed milk than foam.
- Pour over espresso and stir gently if desired.

Quick Tip/Variation

- Great choice for latte lovers who want a cappuccino with extra creaminess.

White Mocha Almond Cappuccino

- Yield: 1 cup (6 oz / 180 ml)
- Brew Time: ~30 sec
- Froth Time: ~45 sec

Ingredients

- 0.7 oz (20 g) espresso beans (double shot)
- ½ cup (120 ml) milk
- 1 tbsp white chocolate syrup
- ½ tsp almond extract
- Foam topping (from frothed milk)

Instructions

- Select **Espresso Mode → Double Shot** and brew into a cup.
- Stir in white chocolate syrup and almond extract.
- Froth milk until creamy with foam, then pour over espresso.

Quick Tip/Variation

- Garnish with slivered almonds for texture and presentation.

Honey Cinnamon Cappuccino

- Yield: 1 cup (6 oz / 180 ml)
- Brew Time: ~30 sec
- Froth Time: ~45 sec

Ingredients

- 0.7 oz (20 g) espresso beans (double shot)
- ½ cup (120 ml) milk
- 1 tsp honey
- ¼ tsp ground cinnamon

Instructions

- Select **Espresso Mode → Double Shot** and brew into a cup.
- Stir honey and cinnamon into espresso.
- Froth milk to create steamed milk with foam and pour over.

Quick Tip/Variation

- Add a cinnamon stick as a stirrer for both flavor and garnish.

Mocha Madness (Double Chocolate)

- Yield: 1 cup (8 oz / 240 ml)
- Brew Time: ~30 sec
- Froth Time: ~45 sec

Ingredients

- 0.7 oz (20 g) espresso beans (double shot)
- ¾ cup (180 ml) milk
- 1 tbsp chocolate syrup
- 1 tbsp cocoa powder
- Whipped cream (optional)

Instructions

- Select **Espresso Mode → Double Shot** and brew into a mug.
- Stir chocolate syrup and cocoa powder into espresso until smooth.

- Froth milk until creamy and pour over espresso mixture.
- Top with whipped cream if desired.

Quick Tip/Variation

- Sprinkle chocolate shavings for a decadent finish.

Cardamom Cappuccino

- Yield: 1 cup (6 oz / 180 ml)
- Brew Time: ~30 sec
- Froth Time: ~45 sec

Ingredients

- 0.7 oz (20 g) espresso beans (double shot)
- ½ cup (120 ml) milk
- ¼ tsp ground cardamom
- Foam topping from frothed milk

Instructions

- Select **Espresso Mode → Double Shot** and brew into a cup.
- Stir ground cardamom into espresso.
- Froth milk to a cappuccino texture and pour over espresso.

Quick Tip/Variation

- Garnish with a light dusting of cardamom or cinnamon.

Rose Latte (Floral Twist)

- Yield: 1 cup (8 oz / 240 ml)

  Brew Time: ~30 sec

- Froth Time: ~45 sec

Ingredients

- 0.7 oz (20 g) espresso beans (double shot)
- ¾ cup (180 ml) milk
- 1 tsp rose syrup or 2–3 drops rose water

Instructions

- Select **Espresso Mode → Double Shot** and brew into a mug.
- Stir rose syrup into espresso.
- Froth milk until silky and pour over.

Quick Tip/Variation

- Garnish with edible rose petals for elegance.

Lavender Honey Latte

- Yield: 1 cup (8 oz / 240 ml)
- Brew Time: ~30 sec
- Froth Time: ~45 sec

Ingredients

- 0.7 oz (20 g) espresso beans (double shot)
- ¾ cup (180 ml) milk
- 1 tsp honey
- 2–3 drops lavender extract or syrup

Instructions

- Select **Espresso Mode → Double Shot** and brew into a mug.
- Stir honey and lavender into espresso.

- Froth milk until creamy and pour over.

Quick Tip/Variation

- Serve with a sprig of lavender for aroma and presentation.

Vanilla Bean Praline Latte

- Yield: 1 cup (8 oz / 240 ml)
- Brew Time: ~30 sec
- Froth Time: ~45 sec

Ingredients

- 0.7 oz (20 g) espresso beans (double shot)
- ¾ cup (180 ml) milk
- 1 tbsp vanilla syrup
- 1 tbsp praline syrup

Instructions

- Select **Espresso Mode → Double Shot** and brew into a mug.
- Stir in vanilla and praline syrups.
- Froth milk until smooth and pour over.

Quick Tip/Variation

- Garnish with crushed candied pecans for a sweet crunch.

Hazelnut Praline Latte

- Yield: 1 cup (8 oz / 240 ml)
- Brew Time: ~30 sec
- Froth Time: ~45 sec

Ingredients

- 0.7 oz (20 g) espresso beans (double shot)
- ¾ cup (180 ml) milk
- 1 tbsp hazelnut syrup
- 1 tbsp praline syrup

Instructions

- Select **Espresso Mode → Double Shot** and brew into a mug.
- Stir hazelnut and praline syrups into espresso.
- Froth milk until creamy and pour over.

Quick Tip/Variation

- Garnish with crushed hazelnuts or praline pieces for added crunch.

Brown Butter Latte

- Yield: 1 cup (8 oz / 240 ml)
- Brew Time: ~30 sec
- Froth Time: ~45 sec

Ingredients

- 0.7 oz (20 g) espresso beans (double shot)
- ¾ cup (180 ml) milk
- 1 tsp brown butter syrup (or browned butter mixed with sugar)

Instructions

- Select **Espresso Mode → Double Shot** and brew into a mug.
- Stir brown butter syrup into espresso.

- Froth milk until silky and pour over.

Quick Tip/Variation

- Sprinkle with nutmeg for a warm finish.

Irish Cream Latte (Alcohol Optional)

- Yield: 1 cup (8 oz / 240 ml)
- Brew Time: ~30 sec
- Froth Time: ~45 sec

Ingredients

- 0.7 oz (20 g) espresso beans (double shot)
- ¾ cup (180 ml) milk
- 1 tbsp Irish cream syrup
- ½ oz (15 ml) Irish cream liqueur (optional)

Instructions

- Select **Espresso Mode → Double Shot** and brew into a mug.
- Stir in syrup (and liqueur if using).
- Froth milk until creamy and pour over.

Quick Tip/Variation

- Top with whipped cream and cocoa powder for a dessert-style latte.

Tiramisu Latte

- Yield: 1 cup (8 oz / 240 ml)
- Brew Time: ~30 sec
- Froth Time: ~45 sec

Ingredients

- 0.7 oz (20 g) espresso beans (double shot)
- ¾ cup (180 ml) milk
- 1 tbsp mascarpone or tiramisu-flavored syrup
- 1 tsp cocoa powder
- Whipped cream (optional)

Instructions

- Select **Espresso Mode → Double Shot** and brew into a mug.
- Stir in mascarpone or tiramisu syrup.
- Froth milk and pour over the espresso mixture.
- Dust with cocoa powder and top with whipped cream if desired.

Quick Tip/Variation

- Add a ladyfinger cookie on the side for the full tiramisu vibe.

Dalgona Coffee Latte (Whipped Coffee Style)

- Yield: 1 glass (10 oz / 300 ml)
- Brew Time: ~30 sec
- Froth Time: ~3–5 min (hand/whisked froth)

Ingredients

- 0.7 oz (20 g) espresso beans (double shot)

- 2 tbsp instant coffee (for whipped topping)
- 2 tbsp sugar
- 2 tbsp hot water
- ½ cup (120 ml) milk
- Ice cubes (optional)

Instructions

- Select **Espresso Mode → Double Shot** and brew into a mug.
- Whip instant coffee, sugar, and hot water until fluffy and frothy.
- Fill a glass with milk (iced or hot).
- Pour brewed espresso into milk.
- Top with whipped dalgona mixture.

Quick Tip/Variation

- Stir before drinking if you prefer a smooth blend.

Café con Leche Latte (Spanish Style)

- Yield: 1 cup (8 oz / 240 ml)
- Brew Time: ~30 sec
- Froth Time: ~45 sec

Ingredients

- 0.7 oz (20 g) espresso beans (double shot)
- ¾ cup (180 ml) steamed milk

Instructions

- Select **Espresso Mode → Double Shot** and brew into a mug.

- Froth milk lightly, focusing on steamed texture rather than foam.
- Pour milk over espresso in equal parts.

Quick Tip/Variation

- Traditionally served strong; adjust milk to taste.

Café au Lait (French Classic)

- Yield: 1 cup (8 oz / 240 ml)
- Brew Time: ~30 sec
- Froth Time: None

Ingredients

- 0.7 oz (20 g) espresso beans (double shot) or strong drip coffee
- ¾ cup (180 ml) hot milk

Instructions

- Brew espresso or drip coffee into a mug.
- Heat milk without frothing and pour directly over coffee.
- Serve immediately.

Quick Tip/Variation

- Pairs beautifully with croissants or pastries.

Flat White (Australian Style)

- Yield: 1 cup (6 oz / 180 ml)
- Brew Time: ~30 sec
- Froth Time: ~45 sec

Ingredients

- 0.7 oz (20 g) espresso beans (double shot)
- ½ cup (120 ml) milk

Instructions

- Select **Espresso Mode → Double Shot** and brew into a small mug.
- Froth milk into a silky microfoam (not foamy).
- Pour gently over espresso, allowing a smooth surface.

Quick Tip/Variation

- Best made with whole milk for a creamier texture.

Cortado Latte (Strong + Creamy)

- Yield: 1 glass (4 oz / 120 ml)
- Brew Time: ~30 sec
- Froth Time: ~30 sec

Ingredients

- 0.7 oz (20 g) espresso beans (double shot)
- 2 oz (60 ml) steamed milk

Instructions

- Select **Espresso Mode → Double Shot** and brew into a glass.
- Froth a small amount of milk to a steamed texture (little foam).
- Pour equal parts milk and espresso together.

Quick Tip/Variation

- Traditionally served in a small glass with no toppings.

Cappuccino Freddo (Iced Greek Cappuccino)

- Yield: 1 glass (8 oz / 240 ml)
- Brew Time: ~30 sec
- Froth Time: ~2–3 min (cold froth)

Ingredients

- 0.7 oz (20 g) espresso beans (double shot)
- ½ cup (120 ml) cold milk
- ½ cup (120 ml) ice cubes
- 1 tsp sugar (optional)

Instructions

- Select **Espresso Mode → Double Shot** and brew espresso.
- Shake espresso with ice and sugar in a shaker until frothy.
- Cold froth the milk separately.
- Pour espresso into a tall glass with ice and top with cold frothed milk.

Quick Tip/Variation

- Sweeten with vanilla syrup for a modern twist.

Iced Caramel Latte

- Yield: 1 glass (12 oz / 360 ml)
- Brew Time: ~30 sec

- Froth Time: None

Ingredients

- 0.7 oz (20 g) espresso beans (double shot)
- ½ cup (120 ml) cold milk
- 1 tbsp caramel syrup
- ½ cup (120 ml) ice cubes

Instructions

- Select **Espresso Mode → Double Shot** and brew espresso.
- Fill a tall glass with ice and pour espresso over it.
- Add caramel syrup and stir well.
- Top with cold milk.

Quick Tip/Variation

- Drizzle extra caramel down the sides of the glass for café-style flair.

Iced Vanilla Latte

- Yield: 1 glass (12 oz / 360 ml)
- Brew Time: ~30 sec
- Froth Time: None

Ingredients

- 0.7 oz (20 g) espresso beans (double shot)
- ½ cup (120 ml) cold milk
- 1 tbsp vanilla syrup
- ½ cup (120 ml) ice cubes

Instructions

- Select **Espresso Mode → Double Shot** and brew espresso.
- Pour espresso into a tall glass filled with ice.
- Add vanilla syrup and top with cold milk.
- Stir gently.

Quick Tip/Variation

- Use vanilla almond milk for a dairy-free twist.

Iced Mocha Latte

- Yield: 1 glass (12 oz / 360 ml)
- Brew Time: ~30 sec
- Froth Time: None

Ingredients

- 0.7 oz (20 g) espresso beans (double shot)
- ½ cup (120 ml) cold milk
- 1 tbsp chocolate syrup
- ½ cup (120 ml) ice cubes
- Whipped cream (optional)

Instructions

- Select **Espresso Mode → Double Shot** and brew espresso.
- Stir chocolate syrup into hot espresso until smooth.
- Fill a glass with ice and pour the espresso mixture over it.
- Add cold milk and stir.

- Top with whipped cream if desired.

Quick Tip/Variation

- Garnish with chocolate shavings for presentation.

Iced Brown Sugar Latte

- Yield: 1 glass (12 oz / 360 ml)
- Brew Time: ~30 sec
- Froth Time: None

Ingredients

- 0.7 oz (20 g) espresso beans (double shot)
- ½ cup (120 ml) cold milk
- 1 tbsp brown sugar syrup (or brown sugar dissolved in hot espresso)
- ½ cup (120 ml) ice cubes

Instructions

- Select **Espresso Mode** → **Double Shot** and brew espresso.
- Stir brown sugar syrup into espresso while hot.
- Fill a glass with ice, pour in sweetened espresso, and top with cold milk.

Quick Tip/Variation

- Add a dash of cinnamon for extra warmth.

Iced Honey Oat Latte

- Yield: 1 glass (12 oz / 360 ml)
- Brew Time: ~30 sec
- Froth Time: None

Ingredients

- 0.7 oz (20 g) espresso beans (double shot)
- ½ cup (120 ml) oat milk
- 1 tsp honey
- ½ cup (120 ml) ice cubes

Instructions

- Select **Espresso Mode** → **Double Shot** and brew espresso.
- Stir honey into hot espresso until dissolved.
- Fill a tall glass with ice and pour the espresso mixture over.
- Top with oat milk.

Quick Tip/Variation

- Sprinkle crushed oats or cinnamon on top for a rustic finish.

Cookie Butter Latte

- Yield: 1 cup (8 oz / 240 ml)
- Brew Time: ~30 sec
- Froth Time: ~45 sec

Ingredients

- 0.7 oz (20 g) espresso beans (double shot)
- ¾ cup (180 ml) milk
- 1 tbsp cookie butter spread or syrup

Instructions

- Select **Espresso Mode** → **Double Shot** and brew into a mug.

- Stir cookie butter into espresso until melted.
- Froth milk until creamy and pour over.

Quick Tip/Variation

- Garnish with crushed speculoos cookies for extra crunch.

Almond Biscotti Latte

- Yield: 1 cup (8 oz / 240 ml)
- Brew Time: ~30 sec
- Froth Time: ~45 sec

Ingredients

- 0.7 oz (20 g) espresso beans (double shot)
- ¾ cup (180 ml) milk
- 1 tsp almond extract
- 1 tsp sugar or almond syrup

Instructions

- Select **Espresso Mode → Double Shot** and brew into a mug.
- Stir almond extract and sugar (or syrup) into espresso.
- Froth milk until silky and pour over.

Quick Tip/Variation

- Serve with an almond biscotti on the side for an authentic pairing.

Toasted Coconut Latte

- Yield: 1 cup (8 oz / 240 ml)
- Brew Time: ~30 sec

- Froth Time: ~45 sec

Ingredients

- 0.7 oz (20 g) espresso beans (double shot)
- ¾ cup (180 ml) milk
- 1 tbsp coconut syrup
- Toasted coconut flakes (optional garnish)

Instructions

- Select **Espresso Mode → Double Shot** and brew into a mug.
- Stir coconut syrup into espresso.
- Froth milk until creamy and pour over.
- Garnish with toasted coconut flakes if desired.

Quick Tip/Variation

- Use coconut milk instead of dairy for an extra tropical flavor.

White Chocolate Raspberry Latte

- Yield: 1 cup (8 oz / 240 ml)
- Brew Time: ~30 sec
- Froth Time: ~45 sec

Ingredients

- 0.7 oz (20 g) espresso beans (double shot)
- ¾ cup (180 ml) milk
- 1 tbsp white chocolate syrup
- ½ tbsp raspberry syrup

Instructions

- Select **Espresso Mode** → **Double Shot** and brew into a mug.

- Stir in white chocolate and raspberry syrups.

- Froth milk until smooth and pour over espresso.

Quick Tip/Variation

- Garnish with fresh raspberries or a drizzle of raspberry sauce.

Chocolate Orange Cappuccino

- Yield: 1 cup (6 oz / 180 ml)

- Brew Time: ~30 sec

- Froth Time: ~45 sec

Ingredients

- 0.7 oz (20 g) espresso beans (double shot)

- ½ cup (120 ml) milk

- 1 tbsp chocolate syrup

- ½ tsp orange zest or orange extract

Instructions

- Select **Espresso Mode** → **Double Shot** and brew into a cappuccino cup.

- Stir chocolate syrup and orange zest into espresso.

- Froth milk to a cappuccino texture and pour over.

Quick Tip/Variation

- Garnish with grated chocolate and a twist of orange peel.

Nutella Latte

- Yield: 1 cup (8 oz / 240 ml)

- Brew Time: ~30 sec

- Froth Time: ~45 sec

Ingredients

- 0.7 oz (20 g) espresso beans (double shot)

- ¾ cup (180 ml) milk

- 1 tbsp Nutella (hazelnut spread)

Instructions

- Select **Espresso Mode** → **Double Shot** and brew into a mug.

- Stir Nutella into espresso until melted and smooth.

- Froth milk until creamy and pour over.

Quick Tip/Variation

- Garnish with a drizzle of Nutella and crushed hazelnuts.

S'mores Cappuccino

- Yield: 1 cup (6 oz / 180 ml)

- Brew Time: ~30 sec

- Froth Time: ~45 sec

Ingredients

- 0.7 oz (20 g) espresso beans (double shot)

- ½ cup (120 ml) milk

- 1 tsp chocolate syrup

- 1 tsp crushed graham cracker

- Whipped cream (optional)
- Mini marshmallows (optional)

Instructions

- Select **Espresso Mode → Double Shot** and brew into a cappuccino cup.
- Stir in chocolate syrup.
- Froth milk to create foam and pour over espresso.
- Top with whipped cream, graham cracker crumbs, and mini marshmallows.

Quick Tip/Variation

- Toast marshmallows for authentic campfire flavor.

Ginger Snap Latte

- Yield: 1 cup (8 oz / 240 ml)
- Brew Time: ~30 sec
- Froth Time: ~45 sec

Ingredients

- 0.7 oz (20 g) espresso beans (double shot)
- ¾ cup (180 ml) milk
- 1 tbsp ginger syrup or molasses
- Pinch of cinnamon and nutmeg

Instructions

- Select **Espresso Mode → Double Shot** and brew into a mug.
- Stir in ginger syrup and spices.
- Froth milk until smooth and pour over.

Quick Tip/Variation

- Garnish with crushed ginger snap cookies.

Horchata Latte (Cinnamon Rice-Inspired)

- Yield: 1 cup (8 oz / 240 ml)
- Brew Time: ~30 sec
- Froth Time: ~45 sec

Ingredients

- 0.7 oz (20 g) espresso beans (double shot)
- ¾ cup (180 ml) milk (or rice milk for authenticity)
- 1 tsp cinnamon sugar
- ½ tsp vanilla extract

Instructions

- Select **Espresso Mode → Double Shot** and brew into a mug.
- Stir cinnamon sugar and vanilla into espresso.
- Froth milk (or rice milk) until creamy and pour over.

Quick Tip/Variation

- Dust with extra cinnamon for a true horchata finish.

Dairy-Free Almond Milk Cappuccino Variations (Mocha, Vanilla, Caramel)

- Yield: 1 cup (6 oz / 180 ml)

- Brew Time: ~30 sec
- Froth Time: ~45 sec

Ingredients (Base)

- 0.7 oz (20 g) espresso beans (double shot)
- ½ cup (120 ml) almond milk

Instructions

- Select **Espresso Mode → Double Shot** and brew into a cappuccino cup.
- Froth almond milk until airy with foam.
- Pour over espresso.
- Add one of the following syrups for variation:
  - ❖ 1 tbsp chocolate syrup (Mocha)
  - ❖ 1 tbsp vanilla syrup (Vanilla)
  - ❖ 1 tbsp caramel syrup (Caramel)

Quick Tip/Variation

- Use barista-style almond milk for a creamier froth.

Your Café Notes

COLD BREWS & ICED COFFEES

Classic Cold Brew

- Yield: 2 cups (16 oz / 480 ml)
- Brew Time: ~10–15 min
- Froth Time: None

Ingredients

- 1 oz (28 g) coffee beans (medium–coarse grind)
- 2 cups (480 ml) cold water
- Ice cubes

Instructions

- Grind beans to medium–coarse and load into hopper.
- Fill the reservoir with cold water.
- Place a tall carafe with ice under the spout.
- Select **Cold Brew Mode** and brew.
- Stir gently before serving.

Quick Tip/Variation

- Add a splash of cream or vanilla syrup for a smoother finish.

Cold Pressed Espresso

- Yield: 1 glass (6 oz / 180 ml)
- Brew Time: ~90 sec
- Froth Time: None

Ingredients

- 0.7 oz (20 g) espresso beans (fine grind, double shot)

- ½ cup (120 ml) cold water
- Ice cubes

Instructions

- Grind beans to a fine, tamp evenly, and lock the portafilter.
- Fill the reservoir with cold water.
- Place the glass with ice under the spout.
- Select **Cold Pressed Espresso Mode** and brew directly over ice.

Premier vs Pro Note

- Pro offers slightly finer temperature control, giving a smoother finish.

Quick Tip/Variation

- Add caramel syrup or vanilla for a café-style twist.

Iced Honey Oat Milk Coffee

- Yield: 1 glass (12 oz / 360 ml)
- Brew Time: ~30 sec
- Froth Time: None

Ingredients

- 0.7 oz (20 g) espresso beans (fine grind, double shot)
- ½ cup (120 ml) oat milk
- 1 tsp honey
- ½ cup (120 ml) ice cubes

Instructions

- Grind beans to a fine and brew a **double espresso shot**.
- Stir honey into hot espresso until dissolved.
- Fill a tall glass with ice.
- Pour espresso mixture over ice and top with oat milk.
- Stir gently to combine.

Quick Tip/Variation

- Garnish with a drizzle of honey along the glass rim.

Spiced Apple Pie Cold Brew

- Yield: 1 glass (12 oz / 360 ml)
- Brew Time: ~10–15 min
- Froth Time: None

Ingredients

- 0.7 oz (20 g) coffee beans (medium–coarse grind)
- 1 tbsp apple syrup or apple juice concentrate
- ¼ tsp ground cinnamon
- Ice cubes

Instructions

- Grind beans to medium–coarse and load into hopper.
- Fill the reservoir with cold water.
- Place the glass with ice under the spout.
- Select **Cold Brew Mode** and brew concentrate.
- Stir in apple syrup and cinnamon until blended.

Quick Tip/Variation

- Garnish with an apple slice and cinnamon stick for a cozy touch.

Vanilla Citrus Cold Brew Fizz

- Yield: 1 glass (12 oz / 360 ml)
- Brew Time: ~10–15 min
- Froth Time: None

Ingredients

- 0.7 oz (20 g) coffee beans (medium–coarse grind)
- 1 tsp vanilla syrup
- 2 tbsp fresh orange juice
- Sparkling water to top
- Ice cubes

Instructions

- Grind beans to medium–coarse and load into hopper.
- Fill the reservoir with cold water.
- Place the glass with ice under the spout.
- Select **Cold Brew Mode** and brew concentrate.
- Stir in vanilla syrup and orange juice.
- Top with sparkling water and stir lightly.

- Swap orange juice with lemon for a sharper citrus kick.

Iced Mocha

- Yield: 1 glass (12 oz / 360 ml)
- Brew Time: ~30 sec
- Froth Time: None

Ingredients

- 0.7 oz (20 g) espresso beans (fine grind, double shot)
- ½ cup (120 ml) cold milk
- 1 tbsp chocolate syrup
- ½ cup (120 ml) ice cubes
- Whipped cream (optional)

Instructions

- Grind beans to a fine and brew a **double espresso shot**.
- Stir chocolate syrup into espresso until smooth.
- Fill a tall glass with ice, pour the espresso mixture over.
- Top with cold milk and stir gently.
- Add whipped cream if desired.

Quick Tip/Variation

- Garnish with chocolate shavings or drizzle for a café-style finish.

Summer Citrus Iced Coffee

- Yield: 1 glass (12 oz / 360 ml)

- Brew Time: ~10–15 min
- Froth Time: None

Ingredients

- 0.7 oz (20 g) coffee beans (medium–coarse grind)
- 2 tbsp fresh lemon juice
- 1 tsp honey or simple syrup
- Ice cubes

Instructions

- Grind beans to medium–coarse and brew using **Cold Brew Mode**.
- Pour concentrate over ice in a tall glass.
- Stir in lemon juice and honey until well blended.
- Top with a splash of water if desired.

Quick Tip/Variation

- Swap lemon with lime juice for a sharper citrus twist.

Kyoto Vanilla Brew

- Yield: 1 glass (12 oz / 360 ml)
- Brew Time: ~10–15 min
- Froth Time: None

Ingredients

- 0.7 oz (20 g) coffee beans (medium–coarse grind)
- 1 tsp vanilla syrup
- Ice cubes

Instructions

- Grind beans to medium–coarse and brew using **Cold Brew Mode**.

- Pour concentrate into a glass filled with ice.

- Stir in vanilla syrup.

- Add extra cold water to adjust the strength if needed.

Quick Tip/Variation

- A dash of cinnamon blends beautifully with the vanilla.

Coconut Cold Press

- Yield: 1 glass (12 oz / 360 ml)

- Brew Time: ~10–15 min

- Froth Time: None

Ingredients

- 0.7 oz (20 g) coffee beans (medium–coarse grind)

- ½ cup (120 ml) coconut milk

- 1 tsp coconut syrup (optional)

- Ice cubes

Instructions

- Grind beans to medium–coarse and brew using **Cold Brew Mode**.

- Pour concentrate over ice in a glass.

- Stir in coconut milk and coconut syrup if using.

Quick Tip/Variation

- Toasted coconut flakes make a nice garnish.

Nitro-Style Cold Brew

- Yield: 1 glass (12 oz / 360 ml)

- Brew Time: ~10–15 min

- Froth Time: ~30 sec (cold foam optional)

Ingredients

- 0.7 oz (20 g) coffee beans (medium–coarse grind)

- ½ cup (120 ml) cold water

- Ice cubes

Instructions

- Grind beans to medium–coarse and brew using **Cold Brew Mode**.

- Pour concentrate into a tall glass filled with ice.

- For a nitro-style texture, use the frother on **Cold Foam Mode** and top the drink.

Quick Tip/Variation

- Vanilla syrup pairs well with the creamy cold foam.

Gingerbread Cold Foam Cold Brew

- Yield: 1 glass (12 oz / 360 ml)

- Brew Time: ~10–15 min

- Froth Time: ~30 sec (cold foam)

Ingredients

- 0.7 oz (20 g) coffee beans (medium–coarse grind)

- 1 tbsp gingerbread syrup

- ½ cup (120 ml) milk (for cold foam)
- Ice cubes

Instructions

- Grind beans to medium–coarse and brew using **Cold Brew Mode**.
- Pour concentrate over ice in a tall glass.
- Froth milk on **Cold Foam Mode**.
- Stir gingerbread syrup into cold brew and top with cold foam.

Quick Tip/Variation

- Sprinkle nutmeg or crushed ginger cookies on top for garnish.

Lavender Honey Cold Brew

- Yield: 1 glass (12 oz / 360 ml)
- Brew Time: ~10–15 min
- Froth Time: None

Ingredients

- 0.7 oz (20 g) coffee beans (medium–coarse grind)
- 1 tsp honey
- 2–3 drops lavender syrup or extract
- Ice cubes

Instructions

- Grind beans to medium–coarse and brew using **Cold Brew Mode**.
- Pour concentrate over ice.
- Stir in honey until dissolved.
- Add lavender syrup and stir gently.

Quick Tip/Variation

- Garnish with a sprig of lavender for a café-style touch.

Iced Brown Sugar Shaken Coffee

- Yield: 1 glass (12 oz / 360 ml)
- Brew Time: ~30 sec
- Froth Time: None

Ingredients

- 0.7 oz (20 g) espresso beans (fine grind, double shot)
- 1 tbsp brown sugar syrup (or brown sugar dissolved in hot espresso)
- ½ cup (120 ml) cold milk
- Ice cubes

Instructions

- Grind beans to a fine and brew a **double espresso shot**.
- Stir brown sugar syrup into hot espresso until dissolved.
- Add espresso, milk, and ice into a shaker.
- Shake vigorously until chilled and foamy.
- Pour into a tall glass.

Quick Tip/Variation

- Add a dash of cinnamon to the shaker for a warm spice note.

Peppermint Mocha Cold Brew

- Yield: 1 glass (12 oz / 360 ml)
- Brew Time: ~10–15 min
- Froth Time: None

Ingredients

- 0.7 oz (20 g) coffee beans (medium–coarse grind)
- 1 tbsp chocolate syrup
- 2–3 drops peppermint extract or 1 tsp peppermint syrup
- Ice cubes

Instructions

- Grind beans to medium–coarse and brew using **Cold Brew Mode**.
- Pour concentrate over ice.
- Stir in chocolate syrup and peppermint extract until well blended.

Quick Tip/Variation

- Garnish with whipped cream and crushed candy cane pieces for a festive finish.

Cinnamon Roll Iced Coffee

- Yield: 1 glass (12 oz / 360 ml)
- Brew Time: ~30 sec (espresso) or 10–15 min (cold brew)
- Froth Time: None

Ingredients

- 0.7 oz (20 g) espresso beans (fine grind, double shot) OR medium–coarse grind for cold brew

- 1 tsp cinnamon syrup
- 1 tsp vanilla syrup
- ½ cup (120 ml) cold milk
- Ice cubes

Instructions

- Brew a **double espresso** or prepare cold brew using **Cold Brew Mode**.
- Pour coffee over ice in a tall glass.
- Stir in cinnamon and vanilla syrups.
- Top with milk and stir gently.

Quick Tip/Variation

- Add whipped cream and a dusting of cinnamon sugar for dessert-style flair.

Salted Caramel Cold Brew

- Yield: 1 glass (12 oz / 360 ml)
- Brew Time: ~10–15 min
- Froth Time: None

Ingredients

- 0.7 oz (20 g) coffee beans (medium–coarse grind)
- 1 tbsp caramel syrup
- Pinch of sea salt
- ½ cup (120 ml) cold milk or cream
- Ice cubes

Instructions

- Grind beans to medium–coarse and brew using **Cold Brew Mode**.
- Pour concentrate over ice in a tall glass.

- Stir in caramel syrup and sea salt.

- Top with milk or cream and stir gently.

Quick Tip/Variation

- Drizzle caramel on top for a sweeter finish.

Toasted Almond Iced Coffee

- Yield: 1 glass (12 oz / 360 ml)

- Brew Time: ~30 sec (espresso) or 10–15 min (cold brew)

- Froth Time: None

Ingredients

- 0.7 oz (20 g) espresso beans (fine grind, double shot) or medium–coarse grind for cold brew

- 1 tsp almond syrup or almond extract

- ½ cup (120 ml) cold milk

- Ice cubes

Instructions

- Brew a **double espresso** or prepare cold brew concentrate.

- Pour coffee over ice in a tall glass.

- Stir in almond syrup or extract.

- Add milk and stir gently.

Quick Tip/Variation

- Garnish with crushed toasted almonds for added crunch.

Maple Pecan Cold Brew

- Yield: 1 glass (12 oz / 360 ml)

- Brew Time: ~10–15 min

- Froth Time: None

Ingredients

- 0.7 oz (20 g) coffee beans (medium–coarse grind)

- 1 tbsp maple syrup

- ½ tsp pecan syrup or extract

- Ice cubes

Instructions

- Grind beans to medium–coarse and brew using **Cold Brew Mode**.

- Pour concentrate into a glass of ice.

- Stir in maple syrup and pecan extract.

Quick Tip/Variation

- Garnish with chopped candied pecans for sweetness.

Honey Cinnamon Iced Latte (Cold Brew Base)

- Yield: 1 glass (12 oz / 360 ml)

- Brew Time: ~10–15 min

- Froth Time: None

Ingredients

- 0.7 oz (20 g) coffee beans (medium–coarse grind)

- 1 tsp honey

- ¼ tsp ground cinnamon

- ½ cup (120 ml) cold milk

- Ice cubes

Instructions

- Grind beans to medium–coarse and brew using **Cold Brew Mode**.
- Pour concentrate over ice.
- Stir in honey and cinnamon.
- Top with milk and stir.

Quick Tip/Variation

- Add a cinnamon stick for extra aroma.

Vanilla Sweet Cream Cold Brew

- Yield: 1 glass (12 oz / 360 ml)
- Brew Time: ~10–15 min
- Froth Time: ~30 sec (cold foam)

Ingredients

- 0.7 oz (20 g) coffee beans (medium–coarse grind)
- 1 tsp vanilla syrup
- ¼ cup (60 ml) heavy cream or half-and-half
- Ice cubes

Instructions

- Grind beans to medium–coarse and brew using **Cold Brew Mode**.
- Pour concentrate into a glass filled with ice.
- Stir in vanilla syrup.
- Froth cream on **Cold Foam Mode** and spoon over cold brew.

Quick Tip/Variation

- For a lighter version, use vanilla almond milk in place of cream.

Mocha Coconut Cold Brew

- Yield: 1 glass (12 oz / 360 ml)
- Brew Time: ~10–15 min
- Froth Time: None

Ingredients

- 0.7 oz (20 g) coffee beans (medium–coarse grind)
- 1 tbsp chocolate syrup
- ½ cup (120 ml) coconut milk
- Ice cubes

Instructions

- Grind beans to medium–coarse and brew using **Cold Brew Mode**.
- Pour concentrate into a glass of ice.
- Stir in chocolate syrup.
- Top with coconut milk and stir gently.

Quick Tip/Variation

- Garnish with toasted coconut flakes for texture.

Chocolate Orange Iced Coffee

- Yield: 1 glass (12 oz / 360 ml)
- Brew Time: ~30 sec (espresso) or 10–15 min (cold brew)
- Froth Time: None

Ingredients

- 0.7 oz (20 g) espresso beans (fine grind, double shot) or medium–coarse grind for cold brew
- 1 tbsp chocolate syrup
- ½ tsp orange extract or zest
- Ice cubes

Instructions

- Brew a **double espresso** or prepare cold brew concentrate.
- Pour coffee into a glass with ice.
- Stir in chocolate syrup and orange extract.

Quick Tip/Variation

- Garnish with an orange peel twist and cocoa dusting.

Almond Biscotti Cold Brew

- Yield: 1 glass (12 oz / 360 ml)
- Brew Time: ~10–15 min
- Froth Time: None

Ingredients

- 0.7 oz (20 g) coffee beans (medium–coarse grind)
- 1 tsp almond syrup
- ½ cup (120 ml) cold milk
- Ice cubes

Instructions

- Grind beans to medium–coarse and brew using **Cold Brew Mode**.
- Pour concentrate into a glass of ice.
- Stir in almond syrup.

- Add milk and stir gently.

Quick Tip/Variation

- Serve with an almond biscotti for dipping.

Pistachio Cream Cold Brew

- Yield: 1 glass (12 oz / 360 ml)
- Brew Time: ~10–15 min
- Froth Time: ~30 sec (cold foam)

Ingredients

- 0.7 oz (20 g) coffee beans (medium–coarse grind)
- 1 tsp pistachio syrup
- ¼ cup (60 ml) heavy cream or half-and-half
- Ice cubes

Instructions

- Grind beans to medium–coarse and brew using **Cold Brew Mode**.
- Pour concentrate over ice.
- Stir in pistachio syrup.
- Froth cream on **Cold Foam Mode** and spoon over cold brew.

Quick Tip/Variation

- Sprinkle crushed pistachios on top for garnish.

Caramel Crunch Iced Coffee

- Yield: 1 glass (12 oz / 360 ml)
- Brew Time: ~30 sec (espresso) or 10–15 min (cold brew)

- Froth Time: None

Ingredients

- 0.7 oz (20 g) espresso beans (fine grind, double shot) or medium–coarse grind for cold brew

- 1 tbsp caramel syrup

- ½ cup (120 ml) cold milk

- 1 tsp crushed caramel candy or toffee bits

- Ice cubes

Instructions

- Brew a **double espresso** or prepare cold brew concentrate.

- Pour coffee over ice in a tall glass.

- Stir in caramel syrup.

- Add milk and top with caramel bits.

Quick Tip/Variation

- Drizzle extra caramel syrup for layered sweetness.

Strawberry Espresso Cold Brew

- Yield: 1 glass (12 oz / 360 ml)

- Brew Time: ~10–15 min

- Froth Time: None

Ingredients

- 0.7 oz (20 g) coffee beans (medium–coarse grind)

- 2 tbsp strawberry puree or syrup

- ½ cup (120 ml) cold milk

- Ice cubes

Instructions

- Grind beans to medium–coarse and brew using **Cold Brew Mode**.

- Pour concentrate into a glass with ice.

- Stir in strawberry puree until blended.

- Add milk and stir gently.

Quick Tip/Variation

- Garnish with fresh strawberry slices for a fruity touch.

Cookies & Cream Cold Brew

- Yield: 1 glass (12 oz / 360 ml)

- Brew Time: ~10–15 min

- Froth Time: ~30 sec (cold foam)

Ingredients

- 0.7 oz (20 g) coffee beans (medium–coarse grind)

- 1 tbsp chocolate syrup

- ¼ cup (60 ml) cream or milk

- 1 crushed chocolate sandwich cookie

- Ice cubes

Instructions

- Grind beans to medium–coarse and brew using **Cold Brew Mode**.

- Pour concentrate over ice.

- Stir in chocolate syrup.

- Froth cream or milk on **Cold Foam Mode** and spoon on top.

- Sprinkle crushed cookie over foam.

- Blend the cookie into the cold foam for extra flavor.

Peanut Butter Mocha Iced Coffee

- Yield: 1 glass (12 oz / 360 ml)
- Brew Time: ~30 sec (espresso)
- Froth Time: None

Ingredients

- 0.7 oz (20 g) espresso beans (fine grind, double shot)
- 1 tbsp peanut butter (smooth)
- 1 tbsp chocolate syrup
- ½ cup (120 ml) cold milk
- Ice cubes

Instructions

- Brew a **double espresso shot**.
- Stir peanut butter and chocolate syrup into hot espresso until smooth.
- Pour mixture over ice in a tall glass.
- Add cold milk and stir gently.

Quick Tip/Variation

- Use peanut butter powder for easier mixing.

Coconut Mocha Iced Brew

- Yield: 1 glass (12 oz / 360 ml)
- Brew Time: ~10–15 min
- Froth Time: None

Ingredients

- 0.7 oz (20 g) coffee beans (medium–coarse grind)
- 1 tbsp chocolate syrup
- ½ cup (120 ml) coconut milk
- Ice cubes

Instructions

- Grind beans to medium–coarse and brew using **Cold Brew Mode**.
- Pour concentrate into a glass of ice.
- Stir in chocolate syrup.
- Add coconut milk and stir gently.

Quick Tip/Variation

- Garnish with toasted coconut and a drizzle of chocolate.

Frozen S'mores Cold Brew

- Yield: 1 glass (12 oz / 360 ml)
- Brew Time: ~10–15 min + blending
- Froth Time: None

Ingredients

- 0.7 oz (20 g) coffee beans (medium–coarse grind)
- 1 tbsp chocolate syrup
- ½ cup (120 ml) milk
- ½ cup (120 ml) ice cubes
- Whipped cream, graham cracker crumbs, mini marshmallows (for topping)

Instructions

- Grind beans to medium–coarse and brew using **Cold Brew Mode**.

- Pour concentrate into a blender with milk, chocolate syrup, and ice.

- Blend until smooth and pour into a tall glass.

- Top with whipped cream, graham cracker crumbs, and mini marshmallows.

Quick Tip/Variation

- Lightly toast the marshmallows for a campfire-style finish.

Lemon Vanilla Iced Coffee

- Yield: 1 glass (12 oz / 360 ml)

- Brew Time: ~30 sec (espresso) or ~10–15 min (cold brew)

- Froth Time: None

Ingredients

- 0.7 oz (20 g) espresso beans (fine grind, double shot) or medium–coarse grind for cold brew

- 1 tsp vanilla syrup

- 1 tsp fresh lemon juice

- Ice cubes

Instructions

- Brew a **double espresso** or prepare cold brew concentrate.

- Pour coffee over ice in a tall glass.

- Stir in vanilla syrup and lemon juice.

Quick Tip/Variation

- Garnish with a lemon slice for a refreshing twist.

Tropical Mango Cold Brew

- Yield: 1 glass (12 oz / 360 ml)

- Brew Time: ~10–15 min

- Froth Time: None

Ingredients

- 0.7 oz (20 g) coffee beans (medium–coarse grind)

- 2 tbsp mango puree or juice

- Ice cubes

Instructions

- Grind beans to medium–coarse and brew using **Cold Brew Mode**.

- Pour concentrate into a glass with ice.

- Stir in mango puree until blended.

Quick Tip/Variation

- Add a splash of coconut milk for a tropical flavor boost.

Pineapple Coconut Iced Coffee

- Yield: 1 glass (12 oz / 360 ml)

- Brew Time: ~10–15 min

- Froth Time: None

Ingredients

- 0.7 oz (20 g) coffee beans (medium–coarse grind)

- 2 tbsp pineapple juice

- ½ cup (120 ml) coconut milk

- Ice cubes

Instructions

- Grind beans to medium–coarse and brew using **Cold Brew Mode**.

- Pour concentrate over ice in a glass.

- Stir in pineapple juice and coconut milk.

Quick Tip/Variation

- Garnish with a pineapple wedge for presentation.

Watermelon Mint Cold Brew

- Yield: 1 glass (12 oz / 360 ml)

- Brew Time: ~10–15 min

- Froth Time: None

Ingredients

- 0.7 oz (20 g) coffee beans (medium–coarse grind)

- ¼ cup (60 ml) watermelon juice

- 3–4 fresh mint leaves

- Ice cubes

Instructions

- Grind beans to medium–coarse and brew using **Cold Brew Mode**.

- Pour concentrate over ice in a glass.

- Stir in watermelon juice.

- Add mint leaves and lightly muddle for freshness.

Quick Tip/Variation

- Freeze watermelon cubes and use them instead of ice.

Raspberry Mocha Iced Coffee

- Yield: 1 glass (12 oz / 360 ml)

- Brew Time: ~30 sec (espresso) or ~10–15 min (cold brew)

- Froth Time: None

Ingredients

- 0.7 oz (20 g) espresso beans (fine grind, double shot) or medium–coarse grind for cold brew

- 1 tbsp chocolate syrup

- 1 tbsp raspberry syrup

- ½ cup (120 ml) cold milk

- Ice cubes

Instructions

- Brew a **double espresso** or prepare cold brew concentrate.

- Pour coffee over ice in a tall glass.

- Stir in chocolate and raspberry syrups.

- Top with cold milk and stir gently.

Quick Tip/Variation

- Garnish with fresh raspberries or a drizzle of raspberry sauce.

Blueberry Honey Cold Brew

- Yield: 1 glass (12 oz / 360 ml)

- Brew Time: ~10–15 min

- Froth Time: None

Ingredients

- 0.7 oz (20 g) coffee beans (medium–coarse grind)

- 2 tbsp blueberry syrup or puree
- 1 tsp honey
- Ice cubes

Instructions

- Grind beans to medium–coarse and brew using **Cold Brew Mode**.
- Pour concentrate into a tall glass with ice.
- Stir in blueberry syrup and honey until blended.

Quick Tip/Variation

- Garnish with fresh blueberries for a colorful finish.

Peach Iced Espresso Cooler

- Yield: 1 glass (12 oz / 360 ml)
- Brew Time: ~30 sec
- Froth Time: None

Ingredients

- 0.7 oz (20 g) espresso beans (fine grind, double shot)
- 2 tbsp peach puree or syrup
- ½ cup (120 ml) cold water or soda water
- Ice cubes

Instructions

- Grind beans to a fine and brew a **double espresso shot**.
- Pour espresso over ice in a tall glass.
- Stir in peach puree.

- Top with cold water or soda water for a sparkling effect.

Quick Tip/Variation

- Garnish with a peach slice for presentation.

Vietnamese Iced Coffee (Cà Phê Sữa Đá)

- Yield: 1 glass (8 oz / 240 ml)
- Brew Time: ~30 sec (espresso) or ~10–15 min (cold brew)
- Froth Time: None

Ingredients

- 0.7 oz (20 g) espresso beans (fine grind, double shot) or medium–coarse grind for cold brew
- 2 tbsp sweetened condensed milk
- Ice cubes

Instructions

- Brew a **double espresso** or prepare cold brew concentrate.
- Pour hot coffee into a glass and stir in condensed milk until smooth.
- Fill another glass with ice and pour the mixture over.

Quick Tip/Variation

- Use extra condensed milk for a sweeter, authentic flavor.

Thai Iced Coffee (Sweet & Spiced)

- Yield: 1 glass (12 oz / 360 ml)

- Brew Time: ~30 sec (espresso) or ~10–15 min (cold brew)
- Froth Time: None

Ingredients

- 0.7 oz (20 g) espresso beans (fine grind, double shot) or medium–coarse grind for cold brew
- 2 tbsp sweetened condensed milk
- 1 tsp sugar
- 1 pinch cardamom or star anise
- Ice cubes

Instructions

- Brew a **double espresso** or prepare cold brew concentrate.
- Stir in condensed milk, sugar, and spice.
- Pour mixture over ice in a tall glass.

Quick Tip/Variation

- Garnish with a dusting of ground cardamom for aroma.

Spanish Iced Café con Leche

- Yield: 1 glass (12 oz / 360 ml)
- Brew Time: ~30 sec (espresso)
- Froth Time: None

Ingredients

- 0.7 oz (20 g) espresso beans (fine grind, double shot)
- ½ cup (120 ml) cold milk
- 1 tsp sugar (optional)
- Ice cubes

Instructions

- Grind beans to a fine and brew a **double espresso shot**.
- Pour espresso into a glass filled with ice.
- Add milk and sugar (if using), stir to combine.

Quick Tip/Variation

- Traditionally strong — adjust milk to taste for a creamier version.

Italian Affogato Cold Brew

- Yield: 1 glass (8 oz / 240 ml)
- Brew Time: ~10–15 min
- Froth Time: None

Ingredients

- 0.7 oz (20 g) coffee beans (medium–coarse grind)
- 1 scoop vanilla ice cream
- Ice cubes

Instructions

- Grind beans to medium–coarse and brew using **Cold Brew Mode**.
- Pour concentrate over ice cream in a chilled glass.
- Stir lightly for a creamy dessert-style coffee.

Quick Tip/Variation

- Swap vanilla ice cream with hazelnut gelato for extra richness.

Japanese Kyoto-Style Iced Coffee (Slow Drip)

- Yield: 1 glass (10 oz / 300 ml)
- Brew Time: ~10–15 min (machine's cold brew)
- Froth Time: None

Ingredients

- 0.7 oz (20 g) coffee beans (medium–coarse grind)
- 1 cup (240 ml) cold water
- Ice cubes

Instructions

- Grind beans to medium–coarse and brew using **Cold Brew Mode**.
- Pour coffee directly over a tall glass filled with ice to mimic slow-drip flavor clarity.
- Stir gently before serving.

Quick Tip/Variation

- Add a few drops of vanilla for a modern twist.

Irish Cream Iced Coffee (Alcohol Optional)

- Yield: 1 glass (12 oz / 360 ml)
- Brew Time: ~30 sec (espresso) or ~10–15 min (cold brew)
- Froth Time: None

Ingredients

- 0.7 oz (20 g) espresso beans (fine grind, double shot) or medium–coarse grind for cold brew
- 1 tbsp Irish cream syrup
- ½ oz (15 ml) Irish cream liqueur (optional)
- ½ cup (120 ml) cold milk
- Ice cubes

Instructions

- Brew a **double espresso** or prepare cold brew concentrate.
- Pour coffee over ice in a tall glass.
- Stir in Irish cream syrup (and liqueur if using).
- Add milk and stir gently.

Quick Tip/Variation

- Top with whipped cream and cocoa powder for a dessert-style drink.

Bourbon Vanilla Cold Brew (Optional Alcohol)

- Yield: 1 glass (12 oz / 360 ml)
- Brew Time: ~10–15 min
- Froth Time: None

Ingredients

- 0.7 oz (20 g) coffee beans (medium–coarse grind)
- 1 tsp vanilla syrup
- ½ oz (15 ml) bourbon (optional)
- Ice cubes

Instructions

- Grind beans to medium–coarse and brew using **Cold Brew Mode**.

- Pour concentrate over ice.
- Stir in vanilla syrup (and bourbon if using).

Quick Tip/Variation

- Garnish with a vanilla bean or orange peel for extra aroma.

Horchata Iced Coffee (Cinnamon Rice-Inspired)

- Yield: 1 glass (12 oz / 360 ml)
- Brew Time: ~10–15 min
- Froth Time: None

Ingredients

- 0.7 oz (20 g) coffee beans (medium–coarse grind)
- ½ cup (120 ml) rice milk (or regular milk with 1 tsp rice syrup)
- 1 tsp cinnamon sugar
- Ice cubes

Instructions

- Grind beans to medium–coarse and brew using **Cold Brew Mode**.
- Pour concentrate over ice in a tall glass.
- Add rice milk and cinnamon sugar.
- Stir gently until blended.

Quick Tip/Variation

- Garnish with a cinnamon stick for a traditional horchata feel.

Tiramisu Iced Coffee

- Yield: 1 glass (12 oz / 360 ml)
- Brew Time: ~30 sec (espresso) or ~10–15 min (cold brew)
- Froth Time: ~30 sec (optional cold foam)

Ingredients

- 0.7 oz (20 g) espresso beans (fine grind, double shot) or medium–coarse grind for cold brew
- 1 tbsp mascarpone or tiramisu syrup
- 1 tsp cocoa powder
- ½ cup (120 ml) cold milk
- Ice cubes

Instructions

- Brew a **double espresso** or prepare cold brew concentrate.
- Pour coffee into a glass with ice.
- Stir in mascarpone or tiramisu syrup.
- Add milk and stir gently.
- Dust cocoa powder on top (or spoon on cold foam if preferred).

Quick Tip/Variation

- Serve with a ladyfinger cookie for a true tiramisu vibe.

Pumpkin Cream Cold Brew (Seasonal)

- Yield: 1 glass (12 oz / 360 ml)
- Brew Time: ~10–15 min
- Froth Time: ~30 sec (cold foam)

Ingredients

- 0.7 oz (20 g) coffee beans (medium–coarse grind)
- 1 tsp pumpkin puree
- ½ tsp pumpkin spice mix
- ¼ cup (60 ml) cream or milk (for cold foam)
- Ice cubes

Instructions

- Grind beans to medium–coarse and brew using **Cold Brew Mode**.
- Pour concentrate over ice in a tall glass.
- Froth cream with pumpkin puree and pumpkin spice on **Cold Foam Mode**.
- Spoon pumpkin cream foam on top.

Quick Tip/Variation

- Sprinkle extra pumpkin spice over the foam for presentation.

Eggnog Cold Brew (Holiday Favorite)

- Yield: 1 glass (12 oz / 360 ml)
- Brew Time: ~10–15 min
- Froth Time: None

Ingredients

- 0.7 oz (20 g) coffee beans (medium–coarse grind)
- ½ cup (120 ml) eggnog
- Pinch of nutmeg
- Ice cubes

Instructions

- Grind beans to medium–coarse and brew using **Cold Brew Mode**.
- Pour concentrate over ice in a tall glass.
- Top with eggnog and stir gently.
- Sprinkle nutmeg on top.

Quick Tip/Variation

- Add a splash of rum extract for a holiday kick.

S'mores Cold Foam Coffee

- Yield: 1 glass (12 oz / 360 ml)
- Brew Time: ~30 sec (espresso) or ~10–15 min (cold brew)
- Froth Time: ~30 sec (cold foam)

Ingredients

- 0.7 oz (20 g) espresso beans (fine grind, double shot) or medium–coarse grind for cold brew
- 1 tbsp chocolate syrup
- ¼ cup (60 ml) milk or cream (for cold foam)
- Crushed graham crackers and mini marshmallows (for topping)
- Ice cubes

Instructions

- Brew a **double espresso** or prepare cold brew concentrate.
- Pour coffee into a tall glass filled with ice.
- Stir in chocolate syrup.

- Froth milk on **Cold Foam Mode** and spoon over coffee.
- Top with crushed graham crackers and marshmallows.

Quick Tip/Variation

- Toast marshmallows lightly for extra flavor.

Black Forest Cold Brew (Cherry + Chocolate)

- Yield: 1 glass (12 oz / 360 ml)
- Brew Time: ~10–15 min
- Froth Time: None

Ingredients

- 0.7 oz (20 g) coffee beans (medium–coarse grind)
- 1 tbsp chocolate syrup
- 2 tbsp cherry juice or puree
- Ice cubes

Instructions

- Grind beans to medium–coarse and brew using **Cold Brew Mode**.
- Pour concentrate over ice.
- Stir in chocolate syrup and cherry juice until well blended.

Quick Tip/Variation

- Garnish with a cherry on top for a classic Black Forest look.

Your Café Notes

SEASONAL SPECIALS

Caramel Apple Latte

- Yield: 1 mug (12 oz / 360 ml)
- Brew Time: ~30 sec (espresso)
- Froth Time: ~45 sec

Ingredients

- 0.7 oz (20 g) espresso beans (fine grind, double shot)
- 2 tbsp apple cider
- 1 tbsp caramel syrup
- ¾ cup (180 ml) milk

Instructions

- Brew a **double espresso shot**.
- Froth milk with caramel syrup until creamy.
- Pour espresso into a mug with apple cider.
- Top with caramel-frothed milk and stir gently.

Quick Tip/Variation

- Garnish with a drizzle of caramel sauce for café-style flair.

Spiced Harvest Mocha

- Yield: 1 mug (12 oz / 360 ml)
- Brew Time: ~30 sec (espresso)
- Froth Time: ~45 sec

Ingredients

- 0.7 oz (20 g) espresso beans (fine grind, double shot)
- 1 tbsp cocoa powder
- ½ tsp cinnamon
- ¼ tsp nutmeg
- ¾ cup (180 ml) milk
- 1 tsp maple syrup

Instructions

- Brew a **double espresso shot**.
- Froth milk with cocoa, cinnamon, nutmeg, and maple syrup.
- Pour espresso into a mug, then add spiced mocha milk.
- Stir until blended.

Quick Tip/Variation

- Add a marshmallow on top for a cozy autumn treat.

Pecan Pie Latte

- Yield: 1 mug (12 oz / 360 ml)
- Brew Time: ~30 sec (espresso)
- Froth Time: ~45 sec

Ingredients

- 0.7 oz (20 g) espresso beans (fine grind, double shot)
- 1 tbsp pecan syrup (or toasted pecan extract)
- ½ tsp brown sugar
- ¾ cup (180 ml) milk

Instructions

- Brew a **double espresso shot**.

- Froth milk with pecan syrup and brown sugar.

- Pour espresso into a mug, then add pecan-sweet milk.

- Stir gently before serving.

Quick Tip/Variation

- Top with crushed pecans for a pie-like finish.

Gingerbread Latte

- Yield: 1 mug (12 oz / 360 ml)

- Brew Time: ~30 sec (espresso)

- Froth Time: ~45 sec

Ingredients

- 0.7 oz (20 g) espresso beans (fine grind, double shot)

- 1 tbsp gingerbread syrup (or ½ tsp ginger + ½ tsp cinnamon + ½ tsp molasses)

- ¾ cup (180 ml) milk

Instructions

- Brew a **double espresso shot**.

- Froth milk with gingerbread syrup until warm and foamy.

- Pour espresso into a mug and top with spiced milk.

Quick Tip/Variation

- Add a mini gingerbread cookie for festive flair.

Holiday Spiced Latte

- Yield: 1 mug (12 oz / 360 ml)

- Brew Time: ~30 sec (espresso)

- Froth Time: ~45 sec

Ingredients

- 0.7 oz (20 g) espresso beans (fine grind, double shot)

- ½ tsp holiday spice blend (cinnamon, nutmeg, clove)

- 1 tbsp honey or brown sugar

- ¾ cup (180 ml) milk

Instructions

- Brew a **double espresso shot**.

- Froth milk with spice blend and honey.

- Pour espresso into a mug, then add spiced milk.

- Stir gently before sipping.

Quick Tip/Variation

- Dust the top with nutmeg for a holiday touch.

Eggnog Latte

- Yield: 1 mug (12 oz / 360 ml)

- Brew Time: ~30 sec (espresso)

- Froth Time: ~45 sec

Ingredients

- 0.7 oz (20 g) espresso beans (fine grind, double shot)

- ½ cup (120 ml) eggnog
- ½ cup (120 ml) milk
- Pinch of nutmeg

Instructions

- Brew a **double espresso shot**.
- Froth eggnog and milk together until warm and foamy.
- Pour espresso into a mug and top with frothy eggnog blend.
- Sprinkle nutmeg over the foam.

Quick Tip/Variation

- Add a splash of rum extract for a holiday kick.

Eggnog Cappuccino

- Yield: 1 mug (8 oz / 240 ml)
- Brew Time: ~30 sec (espresso)
- Froth Time: ~45 sec

Ingredients

- 0.7 oz (20 g) espresso beans (fine grind, double shot)
- ⅔ cup (160 ml) eggnog
- Pinch of cinnamon

Instructions

- Brew a **double espresso shot**.
- Froth eggnog until thick and foamy.
- Pour espresso into a cup and top with eggnog froth.
- Dust with cinnamon before serving.

Quick Tip/Variation

- Great with dairy-free eggnog alternatives too.

Winter Wonderland Mocha

- Yield: 1 mug (12 oz / 360 ml)
- Brew Time: ~30 sec (espresso)
- Froth Time: ~45 sec

Ingredients

- 0.7 oz (20 g) espresso beans (fine grind, double shot)
- 1 tbsp white chocolate syrup
- ½ tsp peppermint extract
- ¾ cup (180 ml) milk

Instructions

- Brew a **double espresso shot**.
- Froth milk with white chocolate syrup and peppermint extract.
- Pour espresso into a mug and top with frothy white chocolate milk.

Quick Tip/Variation

- Garnish with crushed peppermint candy for extra holiday charm.

Candy Cane Cappuccino

- Yield: 1 mug (8 oz / 240 ml)
- Brew Time: ~30 sec (espresso)
- Froth Time: ~45 sec

Ingredients

- 0.7 oz (20 g) espresso beans (fine grind, double shot)

- 1 tbsp peppermint syrup

- ¾ cup (180 ml) milk

- Crushed candy cane for topping

Instructions

- Brew a **double espresso shot**.

- Froth milk with peppermint syrup until foamy.

- Pour espresso into a cup and top with peppermint milk.

- Sprinkle crushed candy cane on top.

Quick Tip/Variation

- Replace peppermint syrup with chocolate-mint syrup for a richer version.

Peppermint Mocha

- Yield: 1 mug (12 oz / 360 ml)

- Brew Time: ~30 sec (espresso)

- Froth Time: ~45 sec

Ingredients

- 0.7 oz (20 g) espresso beans (fine grind, double shot)

- 1 tbsp cocoa powder or chocolate syrup

- ½ tsp peppermint extract

- ¾ cup (180 ml) milk

Instructions

- Brew a **double espresso shot**.

- Froth milk with cocoa and peppermint extract until creamy.

- Pour espresso into a mug and top with chocolate-peppermint milk.

Quick Tip/Variation

- Add whipped cream and crushed peppermint for a festive finish.

Toasted Marshmallow Mocha

- Yield: 1 mug (12 oz / 360 ml)

- Brew Time: ~30 sec (espresso)

- Froth Time: ~45 sec

Ingredients

- 0.7 oz (20 g) espresso beans (fine grind, double shot)

- 1 tbsp chocolate syrup

- 1 tbsp toasted marshmallow syrup

- ¾ cup (180 ml) milk

- Mini marshmallows (optional topping)

Instructions

- Brew a **double espresso shot**.

- Froth milk with chocolate and toasted marshmallow syrup.

- Pour espresso into a mug and top with frothy mocha milk.

- Add mini marshmallows on top if desired.

Quick Tip/Variation

- Lightly toast marshmallows with a kitchen torch for extra flavor.

Hot Cocoa Espresso Twist

- Yield: 1 mug (10 oz / 300 ml)
- Brew Time: ~30 sec (espresso)
- Froth Time: ~45 sec

Ingredients

- 0.7 oz (20 g) espresso beans (fine grind, double shot)
- 2 tbsp hot cocoa mix
- ¾ cup (180 ml) milk
- Whipped cream (optional topping)

Instructions

- Brew a **double espresso shot**.
- Froth milk with hot cocoa mix until creamy.
- Pour espresso into a mug and top with hot cocoa milk.
- Add whipped cream for a café-style finish.

Quick Tip/Variation

- Stir in a cinnamon stick for a cozy winter feel.

Chestnut Praline Latte

- Yield: 1 mug (12 oz / 360 ml)
- Brew Time: ~30 sec (espresso)
- Froth Time: ~45 sec

Ingredients

- 0.7 oz (20 g) espresso beans (fine grind, double shot)
- 1 tbsp chestnut syrup
- ½ tbsp praline syrup
- ¾ cup (180 ml) milk

Instructions

- Brew a **double espresso shot**.
- Froth milk with chestnut and praline syrup until smooth.
- Pour espresso into a mug and add nutty-sweet milk.

Quick Tip/Variation

- Sprinkle crushed pralines on top for texture.

White Chocolate Peppermint Mocha

- Yield: 1 mug (12 oz / 360 ml)
- Brew Time: ~30 sec (espresso)
- Froth Time: ~45 sec

Ingredients

- 0.7 oz (20 g) espresso beans (fine grind, doublc shot)
- 1 tbsp white chocolate syrup
- ½ tsp peppermint extract
- ¾ cup (180 ml) milk

Instructions

- Brew a **double espresso shot**.
- Froth milk with white chocolate syrup and peppermint extract.
- Pour espresso into a mug and top with peppermint white chocolate milk.

- Add whipped cream and crushed peppermint candy for holiday cheer.

Cranberry Bliss Latte

- Yield: 1 mug (12 oz / 360 ml)
- Brew Time: ~30 sec (espresso)
- Froth Time: ~45 sec

Ingredients

- 0.7 oz (20 g) espresso beans (fine grind, double shot)
- 2 tbsp cranberry syrup or juice concentrate
- 1 tbsp white chocolate syrup
- ¾ cup (180 ml) milk

Instructions

- Brew a **double espresso shot**.
- Froth milk with cranberry syrup and white chocolate syrup.
- Pour espresso into a mug and add cranberry-sweet milk.

Quick Tip/Variation

- Garnish with dried cranberries for a festive finish.

Valentine's Raspberry Mocha

- Yield: 1 mug (12 oz / 360 ml)
- Brew Time: ~30 sec (espresso)
- Froth Time: ~45 sec

Ingredients

- 0.7 oz (20 g) espresso beans (fine grind, double shot)
- 1 tbsp chocolate syrup
- 1 tbsp raspberry syrup
- ¾ cup (180 ml) milk
- Whipped cream (optional topping)

Instructions

- Brew a **double espresso shot**.
- Froth milk with chocolate and raspberry syrup.
- Pour espresso into a mug and add raspberry-chocolate milk.
- Top with whipped cream if desired.

Quick Tip/Variation

- Garnish with fresh raspberries for Valentine's flair.

Red Velvet Latte

- Yield: 1 mug (12 oz / 360 ml)
- Brew Time: ~30 sec (espresso)
- Froth Time: ~45 sec

Ingredients

- 0.7 oz (20 g) espresso beans (fine grind, double shot)
- 1 tbsp cocoa powder
- ½ tsp vanilla extract
- 2–3 drops red food coloring (optional)
- ¾ cup (180 ml) milk

Instructions

- Brew a **double espresso shot**.
- Froth milk with cocoa, vanilla, and red food coloring.
- Pour espresso into a mug and add velvety red cocoa milk.

Quick Tip/Variation

- Top with cream cheese frosting for a true red velvet dessert-style drink.

Rose & Cardamom Latte (Spring Bloom Special)

- Yield: 1 mug (12 oz / 360 ml)
- Brew Time: ~30 sec (espresso)
- Froth Time: ~45 sec

Ingredients

- 0.7 oz (20 g) espresso beans (fine grind, double shot)
- 1 tsp rose syrup
- 1 pinch ground cardamom
- ¾ cup (180 ml) milk

Instructions

- Brew a **double espresso shot**.
- Froth milk with rose syrup and cardamom until creamy.
- Pour espresso into a mug and top with floral-spiced milk.

Quick Tip/Variation

- Garnish with dried rose petals for a springtime presentation.

Lavender Honey Spring Bloom Latte

- Yield: 1 mug (12 oz / 360 ml)
- Brew Time: ~30 sec (espresso)
- Froth Time: ~45 sec

Ingredients

- 0.7 oz (20 g) espresso beans (fine grind, double shot)
- 1 tsp lavender syrup
- 1 tsp honey
- ¾ cup (180 ml) milk

Instructions

- Brew a **double espresso shot**.
- Froth milk with lavender syrup and honey until smooth.
- Pour espresso into a mug and add lavender-honey milk.

Quick Tip/Variation

- Try oat milk for a floral, creamy dairy-free version.

Cherry Blossom Latte

- Yield: 1 mug (12 oz / 360 ml)
- Brew Time: ~30 sec (espresso)
- Froth Time: ~45 sec

Ingredients

- 0.7 oz (20 g) espresso beans (fine grind, double shot)
- 1 tbsp cherry syrup
- ½ tsp almond extract

- ¾ cup (180 ml) milk

Instructions

- Brew a **double espresso shot**.

- Froth milk with cherry syrup and almond extract until creamy.

- Pour espresso into a mug and top with cherry-almond milk.

Quick Tip/Variation

- Garnish with a maraschino cherry for a spring festival feel.

Strawberry Shortcake Latte

- Yield: 1 mug (12 oz / 360 ml)

- Brew Time: ~30 sec (espresso)

- Froth Time: ~45 sec

Ingredients

- 0.7 oz (20 g) espresso beans (fine grind, double shot)

- 1 tbsp strawberry syrup

- 1 tsp vanilla syrup

- ¾ cup (180 ml) milk

- Whipped cream (optional)

Instructions

- Brew a **double espresso shot**.

- Froth milk with strawberry and vanilla syrups.

- Pour espresso into a mug and top with flavored milk.

- Add whipped cream for a dessert-like finish.

Quick Tip/Variation

- Sprinkle crushed shortbread cookies on top for extra texture.

Iced Lemon Blossom Latte

- Yield: 1 glass (12 oz / 360 ml)

- Brew Time: ~30 sec (espresso)

- Froth Time: ~30 sec (cold foam)

Ingredients

- 0.7 oz (20 g) espresso beans (fine grind, double shot)

- 1 tsp lemon syrup or zest

- ½ tsp vanilla syrup

- ½ cup (120 ml) cold milk

- Ice cubes

Instructions

- Brew a **double espresso shot** and let it cool slightly.

- Fill a tall glass with ice and pour espresso over.

- Stir in lemon and vanilla syrups.

- Froth cold milk on **Cold Foam Mode** and spoon on top.

Quick Tip/Variation

- Garnish with a lemon twist for a fresh summer look.

Summer Lemon Cold Brew

- Yield: 1 glass (12 oz / 360 ml)

- Brew Time: ~10–15 min (cold brew mode)

- Froth Time: None

Ingredients

- 0.7 oz (20 g) coffee beans (medium–coarse grind)
- 1 tsp lemon juice
- 1 tsp honey
- Ice cubes

Instructions

- Grind beans to medium–coarse and brew using **Cold Brew Mode**.
- Pour concentrate over ice in a tall glass.
- Stir in lemon juice and honey until blended.

Quick Tip/Variation

- Add a mint sprig for a refreshing summer finish.

Key Lime Pie Iced Latte

- Yield: 1 glass (12 oz / 360 ml)
- Brew Time: ~30 sec (espresso)
- Froth Time: ~30 sec (cold foam)

Ingredients

- 0.7 oz (20 g) espresso beans (fine grind, double shot)
- 1 tbsp lime syrup or juice
- 1 tsp graham cracker crumbs (for topping)
- ½ cup (120 ml) cold milk
- Ice cubes

Instructions

- Brew a **double espresso shot** and let it cool slightly.
- Pour espresso over ice in a tall glass.
- Stir in lime syrup.
- Froth cold milk on **Cold Foam Mode** and spoon on top.
- Sprinkle graham cracker crumbs for a pie-like texture.

Quick Tip/Variation

- Add a touch of vanilla syrup for creamier balance.

Coconut Pineapple Summer Latte

- Yield: 1 mug (12 oz / 360 ml)
- Brew Time: ~30 sec (espresso)
- Froth Time: ~45 sec

Ingredients

- 0.7 oz (20 g) espresso beans (fine grind, double shot)
- 1 tbsp coconut syrup
- 1 tbsp pineapple juice
- ¾ cup (180 ml) milk

Instructions

- Brew a **double espresso shot**.
- Froth milk with coconut syrup and pineapple juice.
- Pour espresso into a mug and top with tropical-flavored milk.

Quick Tip/Variation

- Garnish with toasted coconut flakes for a summer touch.

Mango Cream Cold Brew

- Yield: 1 glass (12 oz / 360 ml)
- Brew Time: ~10–15 min (cold brew mode)
- Froth Time: ~30 sec (cold foam)

Ingredients

- 0.7 oz (20 g) coffee beans (medium–coarse grind)
- 2 tbsp mango puree
- ¼ cup (60 ml) cream or milk (for foam)
- Ice cubes

Instructions

- Grind beans to medium–coarse and brew using **Cold Brew Mode**.
- Pour concentrate over ice in a tall glass.
- Froth cream with mango puree using **Cold Foam Mode**.
- Spoon mango cream over cold brew.

Quick Tip/Variation

- Add a splash of coconut milk for a tropical upgrade.

Tropical Sunset Iced Mocha

- Yield: 1 glass (12 oz / 360 ml)
- Brew Time: ~30 sec (espresso)

- Froth Time: None

Ingredients

- 0.7 oz (20 g) espresso beans (fine grind, double shot)
- 1 tbsp chocolate syrup
- 2 tbsp orange juice
- ½ cup (120 ml) cold milk
- Ice cubes

Instructions

- Brew a **double espresso shot** and let it cool slightly.
- Pour espresso over ice in a tall glass.
- Stir in chocolate syrup and orange juice.
- Top with cold milk and stir gently.

Quick Tip/Variation

- Garnish with an orange slice for a sunset look.

Peach Iced Tea Espresso Cooler

- Yield: 1 glass (12 oz / 360 ml)
- Brew Time: ~30 sec (espresso)
- Froth Time: None

Ingredients

- 0.7 oz (20 g) espresso beans (fine grind, double shot)
- ½ cup (120 ml) peach iced tea
- 1 tsp honey (optional)
- Ice cubes

Instructions

- Brew a **double espresso shot** and let it cool.

- Fill a tall glass with ice and pour in peach iced tea.

- Add espresso on top and stir gently.

- Sweeten with honey if desired.

Quick Tip/Variation

- Use sparkling peach iced tea for a fizzy version.

S'mores Latte

- Yield: 1 mug (12 oz / 360 ml)

- Brew Time: ~30 sec (espresso)

- Froth Time: ~45 sec

Ingredients

- 0.7 oz (20 g) espresso beans (fine grind, double shot)

- 1 tbsp chocolate syrup

- 1 tbsp toasted marshmallow syrup

- ¾ cup (180 ml) milk

- Crushed graham crackers (for topping)

Instructions

- Brew a **double espresso shot**.

- Froth milk with chocolate and marshmallow syrups.

- Pour espresso into a mug and top with flavored milk.

- Sprinkle graham cracker crumbs on top.

Quick Tip/Variation

- Add mini marshmallows for a full campfire experience.

Campfire Mocha Shake

- Yield: 1 glass (12 oz / 360 ml)

- Brew Time: ~30 sec (espresso)

- Froth Time: None (blended drink)

Ingredients

- 0.7 oz (20 g) espresso beans (fine grind, double shot)

- 1 tbsp chocolate syrup

- 1 cup (240 ml) milk

- ½ cup (120 ml) ice

- Mini marshmallows and graham crackers (for garnish)

Instructions

- Brew a **double espresso shot** and let it cool slightly.

- Blend espresso, milk, chocolate syrup, and ice until smooth.

- Pour into a tall glass and top with marshmallows and crushed graham.

Quick Tip/Variation

- Use frozen milk cubes instead of ice for a creamier shake.

Fireworks Berry Iced Latte (4th of July Theme)

- Yield: 1 glass (12 oz / 360 ml)

- Brew Time: ~30 sec (espresso)

- Froth Time: ~30 sec (cold foam)

Ingredients

- 0.7 oz (20 g) espresso beans (fine grind, double shot)
- 1 tbsp blueberry syrup
- 1 tbsp strawberry syrup
- ½ cup (120 ml) cold milk
- Ice cubes

Instructions

- Brew a **double espresso shot** and let it cool slightly.
- Fill a tall glass with ice and pour espresso over.
- Stir in blueberry and strawberry syrups.
- Froth milk on **Cold Foam Mode** and spoon on top.

Quick Tip/Variation

- Garnish with red and blue sprinkles for a festive finish.

Autumn Spice Cappuccino

- Yield: 1 mug (8 oz / 240 ml)
- Brew Time: ~30 sec (espresso)
- Froth Time: ~45 sec

Ingredients

- 0.7 oz (20 g) espresso beans (fine grind, double shot)
- ½ tsp pumpkin spice mix (or cinnamon + nutmeg)
- ¾ cup (180 ml) milk

Instructions

- Brew a **double espresso shot**.
- Froth milk with pumpkin spice mix until foamy.
- Pour espresso into a mug and top with spiced milk foam.

Quick Tip/Variation

- Add a drizzle of maple syrup for extra autumn sweetness.

Winter Solstice Spiced Mocha

- Yield: 1 mug (12 oz / 360 ml)
- Brew Time: ~30 sec (espresso)
- Froth Time: ~45 sec

Ingredients

- 0.7 oz (20 g) espresso beans (fine grind, double shot)
- 1 tbsp cocoa powder
- ½ tsp ground clove or allspice
- ¾ cup (180 ml) milk
- 1 tsp brown sugar

Instructions

- Brew a **double espresso shot**.
- Froth milk with cocoa, clove/allspice, and brown sugar until smooth.
- Pour espresso into a mug and add spiced mocha milk.

Quick Tip/Variation

- Garnish with star anise for a wintry aroma.

Springtime Pistachio Latte

- Yield: 1 mug (12 oz / 360 ml)
- Brew Time: ~30 sec (espresso)
- Froth Time: ~45 sec

Ingredients

- 0.7 oz (20 g) espresso beans (fine grind, double shot)
- 1 tbsp pistachio syrup
- ½ tsp vanilla extract
- ¾ cup (180 ml) milk

Instructions

- Brew a **double espresso shot**.
- Froth milk with pistachio syrup and vanilla until creamy.
- Pour espresso into a mug and top with nutty-sweet milk.

Quick Tip/Variation

- Sprinkle crushed pistachios on top for extra crunch.

Summer Strawberry Latte

- Yield: 1 mug (12 oz / 360 ml)
- Brew Time: ~30 sec (espresso)
- Froth Time: ~45 sec

Ingredients

- 0.7 oz (20 g) espresso beans (fine grind, double shot)
- 2 tbsp strawberry puree or syrup
- ¾ cup (180 ml) milk

Instructions

- Brew a **double espresso shot**.
- Froth milk with strawberry syrup until smooth.
- Pour espresso into a mug and top with fruity milk.

Quick Tip/Variation

- Add whipped cream and a fresh strawberry for a summer café vibe.

Your Café Notes

CAFÉ-STYLE DESSERTS & SWEET TREATS

Espresso Tonic

- Yield: 1 glass (10 oz / 300 ml)
- Brew Time: ~30 sec (espresso)
- Froth Time: None

Ingredients

- 0.7 oz (20 g) espresso beans (fine grind, double shot)
- 1 cup (240 ml) chilled tonic water
- Ice cubes
- Lemon slice (optional)

Instructions

- Fill a tall glass with ice.
- Pour chilled tonic water into the glass.
- Slowly brew and pour a **double espresso shot** over the tonic water.
- Garnish with a lemon slice if desired.

Quick Tip/Variation

- For a sweeter taste, add 1 tsp simple syrup.

Tiramisu Latte

- Yield: 1 mug (12 oz / 360 ml)
- Brew Time: ~30 sec (espresso)
- Froth Time: ~45 sec

Ingredients

- 0.7 oz (20 g) espresso beans (fine grind, double shot)
- 1 tbsp mascarpone or tiramisu syrup

- 1 tbsp cocoa powder
- ¾ cup (180 ml) milk
- Whipped cream (optional topping)

Instructions

- Brew a **double espresso shot**.
- Froth milk with mascarpone/tiramisu syrup and cocoa powder.
- Pour espresso into a mug, then top with the tiramisu-flavored milk.
- Add whipped cream for a dessert-style finish.

Quick Tip/Variation

- Dust cocoa powder or crushed ladyfingers on top for authentic flair.

Velvet Mocha Shake

- Yield: 1 glass (12 oz / 360 ml)
- Brew Time: ~30 sec (espresso)
- Froth Time: None (blended drink)

Ingredients

- 0.7 oz (20 g) espresso beans (fine grind, double shot)
- 1 tbsp chocolate syrup
- 1 cup (240 ml) milk
- ½ cup (120 ml) ice
- Whipped cream (optional topping)

Instructions

- Brew a **double espresso shot** and let it cool slightly.

- Blend espresso, milk, chocolate syrup, and ice until smooth.
- Pour into a tall glass.
- Add whipped cream if desired.

Quick Tip/Variation

- Replace chocolate syrup with white chocolate for a twist.

Espresso Affogato

- Yield: 1 glass (6 oz / 180 ml)
- Brew Time: ~30 sec (espresso)
- Froth Time: None

Ingredients

- 0.4 oz (12 g) espresso beans (fine grind, single shot)
- 1 scoop vanilla ice cream

Instructions

- Brew a **single espresso shot**.
- Place ice cream in a small glass or bowl.
- Pour hot espresso directly over the ice cream.

Quick Tip/Variation

- Try hazelnut or caramel ice cream for flavor variations.

Caramel Affogato Sundae

- Yield: 1 glass (8 oz / 240 ml)
- Brew Time: ~30 sec (espresso)
- Froth Time: None

Ingredients

- 0.4 oz (12 g) espresso beans (fine grind, single shot)
- 1 scoop vanilla ice cream
- 1 tbsp caramel sauce
- Whipped cream (optional)

Instructions

- Brew a **single espresso shot**.
- Place ice cream in a dessert glass.
- Pour espresso over the ice cream.
- Drizzle caramel sauce on top.
- Add whipped cream if desired.

Quick Tip/Variation

- Sprinkle crushed toffee bits for crunch.

Iced Churro Latte

- Yield: 1 glass (12 oz / 360 ml)
- Brew Time: ~30 sec (espresso)
- Froth Time: ~30 sec (cold foam)

Ingredients

- 0.7 oz (20 g) espresso beans (fine grind, double shot)
- 1 tbsp caramel syrup
- ½ tsp cinnamon
- ½ cup (120 ml) cold milk
- Ice cubes

Instructions

- Brew a **double espresso shot** and let it cool slightly.

- Fill a tall glass with ice and pour espresso over.

- Stir in caramel syrup and cinnamon.

- Froth milk on **Cold Foam Mode** and spoon on top.

Quick Tip/Variation

- Sprinkle crushed cinnamon-sugar cookies on top for crunch.

Coffee-Glazed Muffin Tops

- Yield: 6 muffin tops

- Brew Time: ~30 sec (espresso, for glaze)

- Froth Time: None

Ingredients

- 1 cup (120 g) all-purpose flour

- ½ cup (100 g) sugar

- ½ tsp baking powder

- ½ cup (120 ml) milk

- 1 egg

- 2 tbsp butter, melted

- 1 shot espresso (for glaze)

- ½ cup (60 g) powdered sugar

Instructions

- Mix flour, sugar, baking powder, milk, egg, and butter into a batter.

- Scoop onto a baking sheet (muffin-top style) and bake at 350°F (175°C) for 12–15 min.

- Brew a **single espresso shot** and whisk with powdered sugar for glaze.

- Drizzle glaze over muffin tops once cooled.

Quick Tip/Variation

- Add chocolate chips to the batter for extra indulgence.

Espresso Shortbread Coins

- Yield: ~24 cookies

- Brew Time: ~30 sec (espresso, for dough)

- Froth Time: None

Ingredients

- 1 cup (225 g) butter, softened

- ½ cup (100 g) sugar

- 2 cups (240 g) all-purpose flour

- 1 shot espresso

- ½ tsp vanilla extract

Instructions

- Cream butter and sugar together.

- Add flour, espresso, and vanilla; mix until dough forms.

- Roll dough into a log, chill, and slice into coin-sized rounds.

- Bake at 350°F (175°C) for 10–12 min until golden.

Quick Tip/Variation

- Dip one side of each cookie in melted chocolate for café flair.

Cinnamon Sugar Donut Bites

- Yield: ~20 bites

- Brew Time: ~30 sec (espresso, optional dipping sauce)
- Froth Time: None

Ingredients

- 1 cup (120 g) all-purpose flour
- 2 tbsp sugar
- ½ tsp baking powder
- 1 egg
- ½ cup (120 ml) milk
- 2 tbsp butter, melted
- ¼ cup sugar + 1 tsp cinnamon (for coating)

Instructions

- Mix flour, sugar, baking powder, egg, milk, and butter into a batter.
- Fry small spoonfuls in hot oil until golden.
- Roll in cinnamon sugar while warm.
- (Optional) Serve with a small shot of espresso for dipping.

Quick Tip/Variation

- Bake instead of frying for a lighter version.

Spiced Mocha Brownies

- Yield: 12 squares
- Brew Time: ~30 sec (espresso, for batter)
- Froth Time: None

Ingredients

- 1 cup (225 g) butter, melted

- 1 cup (200 g) sugar
- 2 eggs
- ½ cup (60 g) cocoa powder
- ½ cup (60 g) flour
- 1 shot espresso
- ½ tsp cinnamon
- ¼ tsp cayenne pepper (optional, for heat)

Instructions

- Mix melted butter, sugar, eggs, cocoa, flour, and espresso into a thick batter.
- Stir in cinnamon (and cayenne if using).
- Bake at 350°F (175°C) for 20–25 min.
- Cool before cutting into squares.

Quick Tip/Variation

- Top with espresso glaze for an extra kick.

Frozen Caramel Coffee Shake

- Yield: 1 glass (12 oz / 360 ml)
- Brew Time: ~30 sec (espresso)
- Froth Time: None (blended drink)

Ingredients

- 0.7 oz (20 g) espresso beans (fine grind, double shot)
- 1 cup (240 ml) milk
- 2 tbsp caramel syrup
- ½ cup (120 ml) ice

- Whipped cream (optional topping)

Instructions

- Brew a **double espresso shot** and let it cool slightly.

- Blend espresso, milk, caramel syrup, and ice until smooth.

- Pour into a tall glass and top with whipped cream if desired.

Quick Tip/Variation

- Drizzle caramel sauce inside the glass before pouring for a café-style look.

Espresso Brownie Bomb

- Yield: 1 dessert glass (serves 2)

- Brew Time: ~30 sec (espresso)

- Froth Time: None

Ingredients

- 0.7 oz (20 g) espresso beans (fine grind, double shot)

- 1 brownie square, chopped

- 1 scoop vanilla ice cream

- 1 tbsp chocolate syrup

Instructions

- Brew a **double espresso shot**.

- Layer chopped brownie in a dessert glass.

- Add a scoop of ice cream.

- Pour hot espresso over the top.

- Drizzle with chocolate syrup.

Quick Tip/Variation

- Use a mocha brownie for double-chocolate intensity.

Cookies & Cream Espresso Shake

- Yield: 1 glass (12 oz / 360 ml)

- Brew Time: ~30 sec (espresso)

- Froth Time: None (blended drink)

Ingredients

- 0.7 oz (20 g) espresso beans (fine grind, double shot)

- 1 cup (240 ml) milk

- 4 chocolate sandwich cookies

- ½ cup (120 ml) ice

- Whipped cream (optional topping)

Instructions

- Brew a **double espresso shot** and let it cool slightly.

- Blend espresso, milk, cookies, and ice until smooth.

- Pour into a tall glass.

- Top with whipped cream if desired.

Quick Tip/Variation

- Crush extra cookies for garnish on top.

Mocha Cheesecake Smoothie

- Yield: 1 glass (12 oz / 360 ml)

- Brew Time: ~30 sec (espresso)

- Froth Time: None (blended drink)

Ingredients

- 0.7 oz (20 g) espresso beans (fine grind, double shot)
- 1 cup (240 ml) milk
- 2 tbsp cream cheese
- 1 tbsp cocoa powder
- ½ cup (120 ml) ice

Instructions

- Brew a **double espresso shot** and let it cool slightly.
- Blend espresso, milk, cream cheese, cocoa powder, and ice until smooth.
- Pour into a tall glass.

Quick Tip/Variation

- Add crushed graham crackers on top for a cheesecake finish.

Espresso Crème Brûlée

- Yield: 4 ramekins
- Brew Time: ~30 sec (espresso)
- Froth Time: None

Ingredients

- 0.7 oz (20 g) espresso beans (fine grind, double shot)
- 2 cups (480 ml) heavy cream
- 4 egg yolks
- ½ cup (100 g) sugar
- 1 tsp vanilla extract
- 2 tbsp sugar (for caramel topping)

Instructions

- Brew a **double espresso shot**.
- Heat cream with espresso until warm.
- Whisk egg yolks, sugar, and vanilla together.
- Slowly stir in warm cream mixture.
- Pour into ramekins and bake in a water bath at 325°F (160°C) for 35–40 min.
- Chill, then sprinkle sugar on top and torch until caramelized.

Quick Tip/Variation

- Add a hint of cinnamon to the custard for a spiced version.

Espresso Pudding Cups

- Yield: 4 small cups
- Brew Time: ~30 sec (espresso)
- Froth Time: None

Ingredients

- 0.7 oz (20 g) espresso beans (fine grind, double shot)
- 2 cups (480 ml) milk
- ½ cup (100 g) sugar
- 3 tbsp cornstarch
- 1 tsp vanilla extract

Instructions

- Brew a **double espresso shot**.
- Heat milk and sugar in a saucepan until warm.

- Stir in espresso, cornstarch slurry, and vanilla.
- Cook until thickened, stirring constantly.
- Pour into cups and chill before serving.

Quick Tip/Variation

- Top with whipped cream and chocolate shavings.

Espresso Éclairs (Quick Version)

- Yield: ~12 éclairs
- Brew Time: ~30 sec (espresso, for filling)
- Froth Time: None

Ingredients

- 1 package pre-baked éclair shells
- 1 cup (240 ml) whipped cream
- 1 tbsp powdered sugar
- 1 shot espresso
- ½ cup (120 g) chocolate glaze

Instructions

- Brew a **single espresso shot** and cool.
- Whip cream with powdered sugar and espresso until thick.
- Fill éclairs with espresso cream.
- Dip tops in chocolate glaze.

Quick Tip/Variation

- Sprinkle crushed nuts for texture.

Coffee Cream Pie Parfaits

- Yield: 4 parfait glasses
- Brew Time: ~30 sec (espresso)
- Froth Time: None

Ingredients

- 0.7 oz (20 g) espresso beans (fine grind, double shot)
- 1 package graham cracker crumbs
- 2 tbsp butter, melted
- 1 cup (240 ml) whipped cream
- 1 cup (240 ml) vanilla pudding

Instructions

- Brew a **double espresso shot** and stir it into vanilla pudding.
- Mix crumbs with butter and press into parfait glasses.
- Layer espresso pudding and whipped cream.
- Chill before serving.

Quick Tip/Variation

- Garnish with chocolate curls or cocoa dust.

Espresso Milkshake Swirl

- Yield: 1 glass (12 oz / 360 ml)
- Brew Time: ~30 sec (espresso)
- Froth Time: None (blended drink)

Ingredients

- 0.7 oz (20 g) espresso beans (fine grind, double shot)

- 2 scoops vanilla ice cream

- 1 cup (240 ml) milk

- 1 tbsp chocolate syrup

Instructions

- Brew a **double espresso shot** and cool slightly.

- Blend espresso, ice cream, and milk until smooth.

- Drizzle chocolate syrup inside the glass.

- Pour shake in and swirl gently.

Quick Tip/Variation

- Use caramel syrup for a caramel swirl twist.

Nutella Mocha Shake

- Yield: 1 glass (12 oz / 360 ml)

- Brew Time: ~30 sec (espresso)

- Froth Time: None (blended drink)

Ingredients

- 0.7 oz (20 g) espresso beans (fine grind, double shot)

- 2 tbsp Nutella

- 1 cup (240 ml) milk

- ½ cup (120 ml) ice

- Whipped cream (optional)

Instructions

- Brew a **double espresso shot** and cool slightly.

- Blend espresso, Nutella, milk, and ice until smooth.

- Pour into a tall glass and top with whipped cream.

Quick Tip/Variation

- Add crushed hazelnuts for crunch.

S'mores Espresso Sundae

- Yield: 1 dessert glass (serves 1–2)

- Brew Time: ~30 sec (espresso)

- Froth Time: None

Ingredients

- 0.4 oz (12 g) espresso beans (fine grind, single shot)

- 1 scoop vanilla ice cream

- 1 tbsp chocolate syrup

- Crushed graham crackers

- Mini marshmallows

Instructions

- Brew a **single espresso shot**.

- Place ice cream in a dessert glass.

- Pour espresso over ice cream.

- Drizzle chocolate syrup and sprinkle graham cracker crumbs.

- Top with mini marshmallows.

Quick Tip/Variation

- Toast marshmallows for an authentic campfire feel.

Black Forest Mocha Shake (Cherry + Chocolate)

- Yield: 1 glass (12 oz / 360 ml)

- Brew Time: ~30 sec (espresso)
- Froth Time: None (blended drink)

Ingredients

- 0.7 oz (20 g) espresso beans (fine grind, double shot)
- 1 cup (240 ml) milk
- 2 tbsp chocolate syrup
- 2 tbsp cherry puree or juice
- ½ cup (120 ml) ice

Instructions

- Brew a **double espresso shot** and let it cool slightly.
- Blend espresso, milk, chocolate syrup, cherry puree, and ice until smooth.
- Pour into a tall glass.

Quick Tip/Variation

- Garnish with whipped cream and a cherry on top.

Toffee Crunch Espresso Shake

- Yield: 1 glass (12 oz / 360 ml)
- Brew Time: ~30 sec (espresso)
- Froth Time: None (blended drink)

Ingredients

- 0.7 oz (20 g) espresso beans (fine grind, double shot)
- 1 cup (240 ml) milk
- 2 tbsp toffee syrup
- ½ cup (120 ml) ice

- Crushed toffee bits (for topping)

Instructions

- Brew a **double espresso shot** and let it cool slightly.
- Blend espresso, milk, toffee syrup, and ice until creamy.
- Pour into a tall glass and top with toffee bits.

Quick Tip/Variation

- Use caramel syrup if toffee syrup is unavailable.

Coconut Cream Mocha Float

- Yield: 1 glass (the 12 oz / 360 ml)
- Brew Time: ~30 sec (espresso)
- Froth Time: None

Ingredients

- 0.7 oz (20 g) espresso beans (fine grind, double shot)
- 1 cup (240 ml) cold milk
- 1 tbsp chocolate syrup
- 1 scoop coconut ice cream

Instructions

- Brew a **double espresso shot** and cool slightly.
- Pour milk and chocolate syrup into a tall glass.
- Add coconut ice cream on top.
- Slowly pour espresso over to create a float.

Quick Tip/Variation

- Sprinkle toasted coconut flakes for added crunch.

Peanut Butter Mocha Shake

- Yield: 1 glass (12 oz / 360 ml)
- Brew Time: ~30 sec (espresso)
- Froth Time: None (blended drink)

Ingredients

- 0.7 oz (20 g) espresso beans (fine grind, double shot)
- 1 cup (240 ml) milk
- 2 tbsp peanut butter
- 1 tbsp chocolate syrup
- ½ cup (120 ml) ice

Instructions

- Brew a **double espresso shot** and cool slightly.
- Blend espresso, milk, peanut butter, chocolate syrup, and ice until smooth.
- Pour into a tall glass.

Quick Tip/Variation

- Use almond butter for a nutty variation.

Frozen Mint Mocha Shake

- Yield: 1 glass (12 oz / 360 ml)
- Brew Time: ~30 sec (espresso)
- Froth Time: None (blended drink)

Ingredients

- 0.7 oz (20 g) espresso beans (fine grind, double shot)
- 1 cup (240 ml) milk
- 2 tbsp chocolate syrup
- ½ tsp peppermint extract
- ½ cup (120 ml) ice

Instructions

- Brew a **double espresso shot** and let it cool slightly.
- Blend espresso, milk, chocolate syrup, peppermint extract, and ice until smooth.
- Pour into a tall glass.

Quick Tip/Variation

- Garnish with whipped cream and chocolate shavings for café flair.

Tiramisu Parfait Cups

- Yield: 4 cups
- Brew Time: ~30 sec (espresso)
- Froth Time: None

Ingredients

- 0.7 oz (20 g) espresso beans (fine grind, double shot)
- 1 cup mascarpone cheese
- 1 cup whipped cream
- 1 tbsp sugar
- Ladyfinger cookies, crushed
- 1 tbsp cocoa powder

Instructions

- Brew a **double espresso shot** and let it cool slightly.

- Mix mascarpone, whipped cream, and sugar until smooth.

- Layer crushed ladyfingers, espresso, and cream mixture in cups.

- Dust with cocoa powder before serving.

Quick Tip/Variation

- Chill for 1–2 hours for firmer texture.

Mocha Ice Cream Sandwiches (Quick Hack)

- Yield: 6 sandwiches

- Brew Time: ~30 sec (espresso, for cream mix)

- Froth Time: None

Ingredients

- 0.7 oz (20 g) espresso beans (fine grind, double shot)

- 12 store-bought chocolate cookies

- 2 cups vanilla ice cream

- 2 tbsp cocoa powder

Instructions

- Brew a **double espresso shot** and cool completely.

- Mix espresso and cocoa into softened ice cream.

- Scoop between two cookies and press gently.

- Freeze until firm.

Quick Tip/Variation

- Roll sandwich edges in mini chocolate chips.

Coffee Biscotti Dippers

- Yield: 12 biscotti

- Brew Time: ~30 sec (espresso, optional glaze)

- Froth Time: None

Ingredients

- 2 cups (240 g) all-purpose flour

- ¾ cup (150 g) sugar

- 2 eggs

- 1 tsp baking powder

- 1 shot espresso (optional, for glaze)

Instructions

- Mix flour, sugar, eggs, and baking powder into the dough.

- Shape into logs and bake at 350°F (175°C) for 20 min.

- Slice into strips and bake again for 10 min until crisp.

- (Optional) Whisk espresso with powdered sugar for a glaze.

Quick Tip/Variation

- Dip ends in melted chocolate for extra crunch.

Espresso Truffle Bites

- Yield: ~20 bites

- Brew Time: ~30 sec (espresso)
- Froth Time: None

Ingredients

- 0.7 oz (20 g) espresso beans (fine grind, double shot)
- 8 oz (225 g) dark chocolate, melted
- ½ cup (120 ml) heavy cream
- 1 tbsp butter
- Cocoa powder (for rolling)

Instructions

- Brew a **double espresso shot**.
- Heat cream and butter, then stir into melted chocolate.
- Mix in espresso and chill until firm.
- Scoop small balls and roll in cocoa powder.

Quick Tip/Variation

- Coat with crushed nuts for variety.

Mocha Fudge Brownie Cups

- Yield: 6 cups
- Brew Time: ~30 sec (espresso, for batter)
- Froth Time: None

Ingredients

- 0.7 oz (20 g) espresso beans (fine grind, double shot)
- 1 cup (225 g) butter, melted
- 1 cup (200 g) sugar
- 2 eggs

- ½ cup (60 g) cocoa powder
- ½ cup (60 g) flour
- ½ cup (60 g) chocolate chips

Instructions

- Brew a **double espresso shot** and stir it into melted butter.
- Mix in sugar, eggs, cocoa powder, flour, and chocolate chips.
- Divide batter into muffin tins.
- Bake at 350°F (175°C) for 20–25 min until set.

Quick Tip/Variation

- Top with espresso glaze for an extra coffee punch.

Choco-Hazelnut Latte Sundae

- Yield: 1 dessert glass (serves 1–2)
- Brew Time: ~30 sec (espresso)
- Froth Time: None

Ingredients

- 0.4 oz (12 g) espresso beans (fine grind, single shot)
- 1 scoop vanilla or hazelnut ice cream
- 1 tbsp Nutella or hazelnut spread
- 1 tbsp chocolate syrup
- Whipped cream (optional)

Instructions

- Brew a **single espresso shot**.
- Place ice cream in a dessert glass.
- Pour espresso over the ice cream.

- Drizzle Nutella and chocolate syrup on top.
- Add whipped cream if desired.

Quick Tip/Variation

- Sprinkle crushed hazelnuts for crunch.

Salted Caramel Espresso Popcorn

- Yield: 8 cups
- Brew Time: ~30 sec (espresso, for caramel)
- Froth Time: None

Ingredients

- 8 cups plain popcorn (air-popped or stovetop)
- 1 cup (200 g) sugar
- ½ cup (120 ml) butter
- ½ cup (120 ml) cream
- 1 shot espresso
- ½ tsp sea salt

Instructions

- Brew a **single espresso shot**.
- Heat sugar and butter until golden brown.
- Stir in cream, espresso, and sea salt.
- Pour caramel over popcorn and toss to coat.
- Spread onto a tray to cool and harden.

Quick Tip/Variation

- Drizzle with melted chocolate for extra indulgence.

Espresso Banana Bread Bites

- Yield: 12 mini bites
- Brew Time: ~30 sec (espresso, for batter)
- Froth Time: None

Ingredients

- 2 ripe bananas, mashed
- 1 cup (120 g) flour
- ½ cup (100 g) sugar
- 1 egg
- 2 tbsp butter, melted
- 1 shot espresso
- ½ tsp baking powder

Instructions

- Brew a **single espresso shot** and stir it into mashed bananas.
- Mix with flour, sugar, egg, butter, and baking powder.
- Divide into mini muffin tins.
- Bake at 350°F (175°C) for 15–18 min.

Quick Tip/Variation

- Add chopped walnuts for crunch.

White Chocolate Raspberry Mocha Shake

- Yield: 1 glass (12 oz / 360 ml)
- Brew Time: ~30 sec (espresso)
- Froth Time: None (blended drink)

Ingredients

- 0.7 oz (20 g) espresso beans (fine grind, double shot)
- 1 cup (240 ml) milk
- 2 tbsp white chocolate syrup
- 2 tbsp raspberry syrup
- ½ cup (120 ml) ice

Instructions

- Brew a **double espresso shot** and let it cool slightly.
- Blend espresso, milk, white chocolate syrup, raspberry syrup, and ice until smooth.
- Pour into a tall glass.

Quick Tip/Variation

- Garnish with whipped cream and fresh raspberries.

Coffee-Almond Bark

- Yield: ~20 pieces
- Brew Time: ~30 sec (espresso, for flavoring)
- Froth Time: None

Ingredients

- 8 oz (225 g) dark chocolate, melted
- 1 shot espresso
- ½ cup (60 g) toasted almonds, chopped

Instructions

- Brew a **single espresso shot** and stir it into melted chocolate.
- Spread chocolate mixture onto a parchment-lined tray.
- Sprinkle toasted almonds evenly on top.
- Chill until firm, then break into pieces.

Quick Tip/Variation

- Add a pinch of sea salt for sweet-salty balance.

Maple Glazed Espresso Donuts

- Yield: 12 mini donuts
- Brew Time: ~30 sec (espresso, for glaze)
- Froth Time: None

Ingredients

- 1 cup (120 g) flour
- ½ cup (100 g) sugar
- ½ tsp baking powder
- 1 egg
- ½ cup (120 ml) milk
- 2 tbsp butter, melted
- 1 shot espresso
- 2 tbsp maple syrup
- ½ cup (60 g) powdered sugar

Instructions

- Mix flour, sugar, baking powder, egg, milk, and butter into a smooth batter.

- Divide into donut pans and bake at 350°F (175°C) for 12–15 min.

- Brew a **single espresso shot** and whisk with maple syrup and powdered sugar for glaze.

- Dip cooled donuts in glaze.

Quick Tip/Variation

- Sprinkle chopped pecans on top for crunch.

Espresso Ice Cream Float (Root Beer or Cola Twist)

- Yield: 1 glass (12 oz / 360 ml)

- Brew Time: ~30 sec (espresso)

- Froth Time: None

Ingredients

- 0.7 oz (20 g) espresso beans (fine grind, double shot)

- 1 scoop vanilla ice cream

- 1 cup (240 ml) root beer or cola

Instructions

- Brew a **double espresso shot** and let it cool slightly.

- Place ice cream in a tall glass.

- Pour root beer or cola over ice cream.

- Slowly add espresso on top.

Quick Tip/Variation

- Try cream soda instead for a sweeter float.

Mocha Cupcake Shake

- Yield: 1 glass (12 oz / 360 ml)

- Brew Time: ~30 sec (espresso)

- Froth Time: None (blended drink)

Ingredients

- 0.7 oz (20 g) espresso beans (fine grind, double shot)

- 1 cup (240 ml) milk

- 1 cupcake (any flavor), crumbled

- 1 tbsp cocoa powder

- ½ cup (120 ml) ice

Instructions

- Brew a **double espresso shot** and let it cool slightly.

- Blend espresso, milk, cupcake, cocoa powder, and ice until smooth.

- Pour into a tall glass.

Quick Tip/Variation

- Use a chocolate cupcake for extra mocha richness.

Coffeehouse Cookie Sandwiches

- Yield: 8 sandwiches

- Brew Time: ~30 sec (espresso, for filling)

- Froth Time: None

Ingredients

- 16 chocolate chip cookies
- 1 cup vanilla ice cream
- 1 shot espresso, cooled
- 2 tbsp cocoa powder

Instructions

- Brew a **single espresso shot** and cool.
- Mix espresso and cocoa into softened ice cream.
- Scoop ice cream between two cookies and press gently.
- Freeze until firm before serving.

Quick Tip/Variation

- Roll sandwich edges in mini chocolate chips for texture.

Your Café Notes

DAIRY-FREE & BLENDED BEAUTIES

Oat Milk Latte

- Yield: 1 mug (12 oz / 360 ml)
- Brew Time: ~30 sec (espresso)
- Froth Time: ~45 sec

Ingredients

- 0.7 oz (20 g) espresso beans (fine grind, double shot)
- ¾ cup (180 ml) oat milk
- 1 tsp maple syrup (optional)

Instructions

- Brew a **double espresso shot**.
- Froth oat milk until creamy and slightly thick.
- Pour espresso into a mug and top with frothed oat milk.
- Stir in maple syrup if desired.

Quick Tip/Variation

- Oat milk froths best when it's barista-style.

Almond Mocha

- Yield: 1 mug (12 oz / 360 ml)
- Brew Time: ~30 sec (espresso)
- Froth Time: ~45 sec

Ingredients

- 0.7 oz (20 g) espresso beans (fine grind, double shot)
- ¾ cup (180 ml) almond milk
- 1 tbsp cocoa powder or chocolate syrup
- ½ tsp almond extract (optional)

Instructions

- Brew a **double espresso shot**.
- Froth almond milk with cocoa powder until smooth.
- Pour espresso into a mug and add the almond-chocolate milk.
- Stir gently to combine.

Quick Tip/Variation

- Top with shaved almonds for texture.

Soy Flat White

- Yield: 1 mug (10 oz / 300 ml)
- Brew Time: ~30 sec (espresso)
- Froth Time: ~30–40 sec

Ingredients

- 0.7 oz (20 g) espresso beans (fine grind, double shot)
- ½ cup (120 ml) soy milk

Instructions

- Brew a **double espresso shot**.
- Froth soy milk lightly to create a thin, velvety foam.
- Pour espresso into a cup and gently add steamed soy milk, holding back most of the foam.

- Soy milk can curdle if overheated — keep frothing temp under 150°F (65°C).

Coconut Iced Coffee

- Yield: 1 glass (12 oz / 360 ml)
- Brew Time: ~10–15 min (cold brew)
- Froth Time: None

Ingredients

- 0.7 oz (20 g) coffee beans (medium–coarse grind)
- ½ cup (120 ml) coconut milk
- 1 tsp coconut syrup (optional)
- Ice cubes

Instructions

- Grind beans to medium–coarse and brew using **Cold Brew Mode**.
- Pour concentrate into a glass of ice.
- Stir in coconut milk and coconut syrup.

Quick Tip/Variation

- Toasted coconut flakes make a great garnish.

Hemp Mocha

- Yield: 1 mug (12 oz / 360 ml)
- Brew Time: ~30 sec (espresso)
- Froth Time: ~45 sec

Ingredients

- 0.7 oz (20 g) espresso beans (fine grind, double shot)
- ¾ cup (180 ml) hemp milk
- 1 tbsp cocoa powder or chocolate syrup
- 1 tsp agave syrup (optional)

Instructions

- Brew a **double espresso shot**.
- Froth hemp milk with cocoa powder until warm and foamy.
- Pour espresso into a mug and add hemp-chocolate milk.
- Sweeten with agave syrup if desired.

Quick Tip/Variation

- Hemp milk adds a nutty undertone perfect for chocolate drinks.

Cashew Chai Latte

- Yield: 1 mug (12 oz / 360 ml)
- Brew Time: ~30 sec (espresso)
- Froth Time: ~45 sec

Ingredients

- 0.7 oz (20 g) espresso beans (fine grind, double shot)
- ¾ cup (180 ml) cashew milk
- ½ tsp chai spice mix (cinnamon, cardamom, ginger, cloves)
- 1 tsp honey (optional)

Instructions

- Brew a **double espresso shot**.

- Froth cashew milk with chai spice and honey.
- Pour espresso into a mug and add spiced cashew milk.

Quick Tip/Variation

- For a stronger chai flavor, steep chai tea in cashew milk before frothing.

Pea Protein Cold Brew

- Yield: 1 glass (12 oz / 360 ml)
- Brew Time: ~10–15 min (cold brew mode)
- Froth Time: None

Ingredients

- 0.7 oz (20 g) coffee beans (medium–coarse grind)
- ½ cup (120 ml) pea protein milk
- 1 tsp cocoa powder (optional)
- Ice cubes

Instructions

- Grind beans to medium–coarse and brew using **Cold Brew Mode**.
- Pour concentrate into a glass filled with ice.
- Stir in pea protein milk (and cocoa if desired).

Quick Tip/Variation

- Great as a post-workout pick-me-up thanks to extra protein.

Strawberry Espresso Milkshake

- Yield: 1 glass (12 oz / 360 ml)
- Brew Time: ~30 sec (espresso)
- Froth Time: None (blended drink)

Ingredients

- 0.7 oz (20 g) espresso beans (fine grind, double shot)
- 1 cup (240 ml) almond or oat milk
- 2 scoops of strawberry ice cream
- ½ cup (120 ml) ice

Instructions

- Brew a **double espresso shot** and let it cool slightly.
- Blend espresso, milk, ice cream, and ice until smooth.
- Pour into a tall glass.

Quick Tip/Variation

- Top with whipped cream and fresh strawberries.

Banana Nut Cold Brew Blast

- Yield: 1 glass (12 oz / 360 ml)
- Brew Time: ~10–15 min (cold brew mode)
- Froth Time: None

Ingredients

- 0.7 oz (20 g) coffee beans (medium–coarse grind)
- ½ banana, sliced

- ½ cup (120 ml) almond or oat milk

- 1 tbsp peanut butter or almond butter

- Ice cubes

Instructions

- Grind beans to medium–coarse and brew using **Cold Brew Mode**.

- In a blender, combine cold brew, banana, nut butter, and milk with ice.

- Blend until smooth and creamy.

Quick Tip/Variation

- Add a scoop of protein powder for an energy boost.

Coconut Cardamom Iced Frappe

- Yield: 1 glass (12 oz / 360 ml)

- Brew Time: ~30 sec (espresso)

- Froth Time: None (blended drink)

Ingredients

- 0.7 oz (20 g) espresso beans (fine grind, double shot)

- 1 cup (240 ml) coconut milk

- ½ tsp ground cardamom

- 1 tbsp sugar or syrup

- ½ cup (120 ml) ice

Instructions

- Brew a **double espresso shot** and cool slightly.

- Blend espresso, coconut milk, cardamom, sugar, and ice until smooth.

- Pour into a tall glass.

Quick Tip/Variation

- Garnish with a pinch of cardamom or toasted coconut flakes.

Dark Chocolate Peanut Butter Frappe

- Yield: 1 glass (12 oz / 360 ml)

- Brew Time: ~30 sec (espresso)

- Froth Time: None (blended drink)

Ingredients

- 0.7 oz (20 g) espresso beans (fine grind, double shot)

- 1 cup (240 ml) almond or oat milk

- 2 tbsp peanut butter

- 2 tbsp dark chocolate syrup

- ½ cup (120 ml) ice

Instructions

- Brew a **double espresso shot** and let it cool slightly.

- Blend espresso, milk, peanut butter, chocolate syrup, and ice until creamy.

- Pour into a tall glass.

Quick Tip/Variation

- Swap peanut butter for almond butter for a nuttier twist.

Almond Butter Cold Brew Shake

- Yield: 1 glass (12 oz / 360 ml)

- Brew Time: ~10–15 min (cold brew mode)
- Froth Time: None

Ingredients

- 0.7 oz (20 g) coffee beans (medium–coarse grind)
- ½ cup (120 ml) almond milk
- 2 tbsp almond butter
- 1 tbsp maple syrup
- ½ cup (120 ml) ice

Instructions

- Brew concentrate using **Cold Brew Mode**.
- Blend cold brew with almond milk, almond butter, maple syrup, and ice.
- Pour into a chilled glass.

Quick Tip/Variation

- Add cacao nibs for texture.

Matcha Oat Milk Latte

- Yield: 1 mug (12 oz / 360 ml)
- Brew Time: None (matcha whisking)
- Froth Time: ~30–40 sec

Ingredients

- 1 tsp matcha powder
- ¼ cup (60 ml) hot water (175°F / 80°C, not boiling)
- ¾ cup (180 ml) oat milk
- 1 tsp honey or agave syrup

Instructions

- Whisk matcha powder with hot water until frothy.
- Froth oat milk until creamy.
- Pour matcha into a mug and top with frothed oat milk.
- Stir in sweetener if desired.

Quick Tip/Variation

- Add a splash of vanilla extract for depth.

Cinnamon Oat Milk Latte

- Yield: 1 mug (12 oz / 360 ml)
- Brew Time: ~30 sec (espresso)
- Froth Time: ~45 sec

Ingredients

- 0.7 oz (20 g) espresso beans (fine grind, double shot)
- ¾ cup (180 ml) oat milk
- ½ tsp ground cinnamon
- 1 tsp maple syrup (optional)

Instructions

- Brew a **double espresso shot**.
- Froth oat milk with cinnamon until lightly thickened.
- Pour espresso into a mug and top with cinnamon oat milk.
- Sweeten with maple syrup if desired.

Quick Tip/Variation

- Sprinkle extra cinnamon on top for aroma.

Vanilla Almond Latte

- Yield: 1 mug (12 oz / 360 ml)
- Brew Time: ~30 sec (espresso)
- Froth Time: ~45 sec

Ingredients

- 0.7 oz (20 g) espresso beans (fine grind, double shot)
- ¾ cup (180 ml) almond milk
- 1 tsp vanilla extract
- 1 tsp sugar or honey

Instructions

- Brew a **double espresso shot**.
- Froth almond milk with vanilla extract.
- Pour espresso into a mug and add frothed vanilla almond milk.
- Stir in sweetener if desired.

Quick Tip/Variation

- Try almond-vanilla syrup for extra café flair.

Coconut Caramel Mocha

- Yield: 1 mug (12 oz / 360 ml)
- Brew Time: ~30 sec (espresso)
- Froth Time: ~45 sec

Ingredients

- 0.7 oz (20 g) espresso beans (fine grind, double shot)
- ¾ cup (180 ml) coconut milk
- 1 tbsp caramel syrup
- 1 tbsp cocoa powder or chocolate syrup

Instructions

- Brew a **double espresso shot**.
- Froth coconut milk with caramel syrup until creamy.
- Stir cocoa into espresso and top with caramel coconut milk.

Quick Tip/Variation

- Garnish with toasted coconut flakes.

Chai Spiced Oat Latte

- Yield: 1 mug (12 oz / 360 ml)
- Brew Time: ~30 sec (espresso)
- Froth Time: ~45 sec

Ingredients

- 0.7 oz (20 g) espresso beans (fine grind, double shot)
- ¾ cup (180 ml) oat milk
- ½ tsp chai spice mix
- 1 tsp honey or agave syrup (optional)

Instructions

- Brew a **double espresso shot**.
- Froth oat milk with chai spice until warm and slightly foamy.
- Pour espresso into a mug and add spiced oat milk.
- Sweeten if desired.

- Stronger chai flavor? Steep a chai tea bag in hot oat milk before frothing.

Mocha Coconut Protein Shake

- Yield: 1 glass (12 oz / 360 ml)
- Brew Time: ~30 sec (espresso)
- Froth Time: None (blended drink)

Ingredients

- 0.7 oz (20 g) espresso beans (fine grind, double shot)
- 1 cup (240 ml) coconut milk
- 1 scoop chocolate protein powder
- 1 tbsp cocoa powder
- ½ cup (120 ml) ice

Instructions

- Brew a **double espresso shot** and cool slightly.
- Blend espresso, coconut milk, protein powder, cocoa, and ice until smooth.
- Serve chilled in a tall glass.

Quick Tip/Variation

- Great pre- or post-workout energizer.

Iced Hazelnut Almond Latte

- Yield: 1 glass (12 oz / 360 ml)
- Brew Time: ~30 sec (espresso)
- Froth Time: None

Ingredients

- 0.7 oz (20 g) espresso beans (fine grind, double shot)
- ¾ cup (180 ml) almond milk
- 1 tbsp hazelnut syrup
- Ice cubes

Instructions

- Brew a **double espresso shot** and let it cool slightly.
- Pour espresso over a glass of ice.
- Stir in almond milk and hazelnut syrup.

Quick Tip/Variation

- Add cocoa powder for a nutty mocha version.

Pistachio Oat Milk Latte

- Yield: 1 mug (12 oz / 360 ml)
- Brew Time: ~30 sec (espresso)
- Froth Time: ~45 sec

Ingredients

- 0.7 oz (20 g) espresso beans (fine grind, double shot)
- ¾ cup (180 ml) oat milk
- 1 tbsp pistachio syrup or paste
- 1 tsp sugar (optional)

Instructions

- Brew a **double espresso shot**.
- Froth oat milk with pistachio syrup until creamy.
- Pour espresso into a mug and add pistachio oat milk.

- Garnish with crushed pistachios on top.

Macadamia Mocha Frappe

- Yield: 1 glass (12 oz / 360 ml)
- Brew Time: ~30 sec (espresso)
- Froth Time: None (blended drink)

Ingredients

- 0.7 oz (20 g) espresso beans (fine grind, double shot)
- 1 cup (240 ml) almond milk
- 2 tbsp macadamia syrup or macadamia butter
- 1 tbsp cocoa powder
- ½ cup (120 ml) ice

Instructions

- Brew a **double espresso shot** and let it cool slightly.
- Blend espresso, almond milk, macadamia syrup, cocoa powder, and ice until smooth.
- Pour into a tall glass.

Quick Tip/Variation

- Top with whipped cream for a rich, creamy finish.

Blueberry Almond Latte

- Yield: 1 mug (12 oz / 360 ml)
- Brew Time: ~30 sec (espresso)
- Froth Time: ~45 sec

Ingredients

- 0.7 oz (20 g) espresso beans (fine grind, double shot)
- ¾ cup (180 ml) almond milk
- 1 tbsp blueberry syrup or blueberry puree
- ½ tsp vanilla extract (optional)

Instructions

- Brew a **double espresso shot**.
- Froth almond milk with blueberry syrup and vanilla extract.
- Pour espresso into a mug and add the blueberry almond milk.

Quick Tip/Variation

- Garnish with fresh blueberries or a few mint leaves for a refreshing twist.

Maple Pecan Oat Milk Latte

- Yield: 1 mug (12 oz / 360 ml)
- Brew Time: ~30 sec (espresso)
- Froth Time: ~45 sec

Ingredients

- 0.7 oz (20 g) espresso beans (fine grind, double shot)
- ¾ cup (180 ml) oat milk
- 1 tbsp maple syrup
- 1 tsp pecan syrup (optional)

Instructions

- Brew a **double espresso shot**.
- Froth oat milk with maple syrup and pecan syrup until thick and creamy.

- Pour espresso into a mug and add the frothy maple-pecan milk.

Quick Tip/Variation

- Top with crushed pecans for extra texture and flavor.

Espresso Almond Protein Smoothie

- Yield: 1 glass (12 oz / 360 ml)
- Brew Time: ~30 sec (espresso)
- Froth Time: None (blended drink)

Ingredients

- 0.7 oz (20 g) espresso beans (fine grind, double shot)
- 1 cup (240 ml) almond milk
- 1 scoop vanilla protein powder
- 1 tbsp almond butter
- ½ banana
- Ice cubes

Instructions

- Brew a **double espresso shot** and cool slightly.
- Blend espresso, almond milk, protein powder, almond butter, banana, and ice until smooth.
- Pour into a tall glass.

Quick Tip/Variation

- Add a few ice cubes of almond milk for an even creamier smoothie.

Mango Coconut Cold Brew Cooler

- Yield: 1 glass (12 oz / 360 ml)
- Brew Time: ~10–15 min (cold brew mode)
- Froth Time: None

Ingredients

- 0.7 oz (20 g) coffee beans (medium–coarse grind)
- 1 tbsp coconut syrup
- 2 tbsp mango puree or syrup
- Ice cubes

Instructions

- Grind beans to medium–coarse and brew using **Cold Brew Mode**.
- Pour concentrate over ice in a tall glass.
- Stir in coconut syrup and mango puree until well blended.

Quick Tip/Variation

- Garnish with a slice of mango or toasted coconut for an extra tropical finish.

Pineapple Espresso Shake

- Yield: 1 glass (12 oz / 360 ml)
- Brew Time: ~30 sec (espresso)
- Froth Time: None (blended drink)

Ingredients

- 0.7 oz (20 g) espresso beans (fine grind, double shot)

- 1 cup (240 ml) coconut milk

- 1/2 cup (120 g) frozen pineapple chunks

- 1 tbsp honey or maple syrup (optional)

- ½ cup (120 ml) ice

Instructions

- Brew a **double espresso shot** and let it cool slightly.

- Blend espresso, coconut milk, pineapple chunks, sweetener, and ice until smooth.

- Pour into a tall glass.

Quick Tip/Variation

- Garnish with a pineapple slice for a tropical touch.

Tropical Coconut Almond Iced Coffee

- Yield: 1 glass (12 oz / 360 ml)

- Brew Time: ~10–15 min (cold brew mode)

- Froth Time: None

Ingredients

- 0.7 oz (20 g) coffee beans (medium–coarse grind)

- 1 tbsp coconut syrup

- ½ cup (120 ml) almond milk

- Ice cubes

Instructions

- Grind beans to medium–coarse and brew using **Cold Brew Mode**.

- Pour concentrate into a glass filled with ice.

- Stir in coconut syrup and almond milk.

Quick Tip/Variation

- Use chilled coconut water for an extra refreshing twist.

Espresso Date Shake (Naturally Sweet)

- Yield: 1 glass (12 oz / 360 ml)

- Brew Time: ~30 sec (espresso)

- Froth Time: None (blended drink)

Ingredients

- 0.7 oz (20 g) espresso beans (fine grind, double shot)

- 3–4 pitted dates

- 1 cup (240 ml) almond or oat milk

- ½ cup (120 ml) ice

Instructions

- Brew a **double espresso shot** and let it cool slightly.

- Blend espresso, dates, milk, and ice until smooth.

- Pour into a tall glass.

Quick Tip/Variation

- Use Medjool dates for a deeper, richer flavor.

Vegan Horchata Latte (Rice & Almond Base)

- Yield: 1 mug (12 oz / 360 ml)
- Brew Time: ~30 sec (espresso)
- Froth Time: ~45 sec

Ingredients

- 0.7 oz (20 g) espresso beans (fine grind, double shot)
- ¾ cup (180 ml) rice milk
- ¼ cup (60 ml) almond milk
- 1 tsp cinnamon
- 1 tsp maple syrup

Instructions

- Brew a **double espresso shot**.
- Froth rice and almond milk with cinnamon until smooth.
- Pour espresso into a mug and top with spiced milk.
- Stir in maple syrup.

Quick Tip/Variation

- Sprinkle extra cinnamon or nutmeg on top for extra flavor.

Plant-Based Gingerbread Latte

- Yield: 1 mug (12 oz / 360 ml)
- Brew Time: ~30 sec (espresso)
- Froth Time: ~45 sec

Ingredients

- 0.7 oz (20 g) espresso beans (fine grind, double shot)
- ¾ cup (180 ml) almond or oat milk
- 1 tbsp molasses
- ½ tsp ground ginger
- ¼ tsp cinnamon

Instructions

- Brew a **double espresso shot**.
- Froth milk with molasses, ginger, and cinnamon.
- Pour espresso into a mug and top with spiced milk.

Quick Tip/Variation

- Garnish with a cinnamon stick for a festive touch.

Almond Chocolate Chip Mocha Shake

- Yield: 1 glass (12 oz / 360 ml)
- Brew Time: ~30 sec (espresso)
- Froth Time: None (blended drink)

Ingredients

- 0.7 oz (20 g) espresso beans (fine grind, double shot)
- 1 cup (240 ml) almond milk
- 2 tbsp chocolate chips (melted)
- 1 tbsp almond butter
- ½ cup (120 ml) ice

Instructions

- Brew a **double espresso shot** and let it cool slightly.

- Blend espresso, almond milk, melted chocolate chips, almond butter, and ice until smooth.

- Pour into a tall glass.

Quick Tip/Variation

- Garnish with a sprinkle of chopped almonds for added texture.

Coconut Matcha Latte

- Yield: 1 mug (12 oz / 360 ml)

- Brew Time: None (matcha whisking)

- Froth Time: ~30–40 sec

Ingredients

- 1 tsp matcha powder

- ¾ cup (180 ml) coconut milk

- 1 tsp maple syrup (optional)

Instructions

- Whisk matcha powder with a splash of hot water until smooth and frothy.

- Froth coconut milk until creamy.

- Pour matcha into a mug and top with coconut milk.

- Stir in maple syrup if desired.

Quick Tip/Variation

- Add a dash of vanilla extract for added depth.

Strawberry Coconut Latte

- Yield: 1 mug (12 oz / 360 ml)

- Brew Time: ~30 sec (espresso)

- Froth Time: ~45 sec

Ingredients

- 0.7 oz (20 g) espresso beans (fine grind, double shot)

- 1 tbsp strawberry puree or syrup

- ¾ cup (180 ml) coconut milk

- 1 tsp sugar (optional)

Instructions

- Brew a **double espresso shot**.

- Froth coconut milk with strawberry puree until smooth.

- Pour espresso into a mug and top with strawberry-coconut milk.

- Sweeten with sugar if desired.

Quick Tip/Variation

- Garnish with fresh strawberry slices for a beautiful presentation.

Espresso Avocado Smoothie (Keto-Friendly)

- Yield: 1 glass (12 oz / 360 ml)

- Brew Time: ~30 sec (espresso)

- Froth Time: None (blended drink)

Ingredients

- 0.7 oz (20 g) espresso beans (fine grind, double shot)

- ½ avocado

- 1 cup (240 ml) unsweetened almond milk

- 1 tbsp coconut oil or MCT oil

- 1–2 ice cubes

Instructions

- Brew a **double espresso shot** and let it cool.

- Blend espresso, avocado, almond milk, coconut oil, and ice until smooth.

- Serve chilled in a tall glass.

Quick Tip/Variation

- Add a few drops of stevia if you prefer extra sweetness.

Dark Cocoa Cashew Mocha

- Yield: 1 mug (12 oz / 360 ml)

- Brew Time: ~30 sec (espresso)

- Froth Time: ~45 sec

Ingredients

- 0.7 oz (20 g) espresso beans (fine grind, double shot)

- 1 tbsp cocoa powder

- ¾ cup (180 ml) cashew milk

- 1 tsp maple syrup (optional)

Instructions

- Brew a **double espresso shot**.

- Froth cashew milk with cocoa powder and maple syrup until smooth.

- Pour espresso into a mug and top with chocolate-cashew milk.

Quick Tip/Variation

- Use cacao powder for a richer chocolate flavor.

Iced Coconut Almond Cream Latte

- Yield: 1 glass (12 oz / 360 ml)

- Brew Time: ~30 sec (espresso)

- Froth Time: ~45 sec

Ingredients

- 0.7 oz (20 g) espresso beans (fine grind, double shot)

- ¾ cup (180 ml) coconut milk

- ¼ cup (60 ml) almond milk

- 1 tbsp honey or maple syrup (optional)

- Ice cubes

Instructions

- Brew a **double espresso shot** and let it cool slightly.

- Froth coconut and almond milk together until creamy.

- Pour espresso over ice in a tall glass.

- Top with the frothy coconut almond milk.

Quick Tip/Variation

- Add a dash of vanilla extract for extra flavor depth.

Almond Biscotti Protein Shake

- Yield: 1 glass (12 oz / 360 ml)

- Brew Time: ~30 sec (espresso)

- Froth Time: None (blended drink)

Ingredients

- 0.7 oz (20 g) espresso beans (fine grind, double shot)
- 1 cup (240 ml) almond milk
- 1 scoop vanilla protein powder
- 2 biscotti cookies (crumbled)
- ½ cup (120 ml) ice

Instructions

- Brew a **double espresso shot** and cool slightly.
- Blend espresso, almond milk, protein powder, biscotti crumbs, and ice until smooth.
- Pour into a tall glass.

Quick Tip/Variation

- Use almond or coconut protein powder for added flavor.

Spiced Almond Butter Mocha Shake

- Yield: 1 glass (12 oz / 360 ml)
- Brew Time: ~30 sec (espresso)
- Froth Time: None (blended drink)

Ingredients

- 0.7 oz (20 g) espresso beans (fine grind, double shot)
- 1 cup (240 ml) almond milk
- 2 tbsp almond butter
- 1 tbsp cocoa powder
- ½ tsp cinnamon
- ½ cup (120 ml) ice

Instructions

- Brew a **double espresso shot** and cool slightly.
- Blend espresso, almond milk, almond butter, cocoa, cinnamon, and ice until smooth.
- Pour into a tall glass.

Quick Tip/Variation

- Top with extra cinnamon or chocolate shavings for garnish.

Oat & Maple Cold Brew Smoothie

- Yield: 1 glass (12 oz / 360 ml)
- Brew Time: ~10–15 min (cold brew mode)
- Froth Time: None

Ingredients

- 0.7 oz (20 g) coffee beans (medium–coarse grind)
- ½ cup (120 ml) oat milk
- 1 tbsp maple syrup
- ½ cup (120 ml) frozen banana
- ½ cup (120 ml) ice

Instructions

- Grind beans to medium–coarse and brew using **Cold Brew Mode**.
- Pour concentrate over ice in a tall glass.

- Blend oat milk, maple syrup, frozen banana, and ice until smooth.
- Pour over cold brew concentrate and stir gently.

Quick Tip/Variation

- Add a scoop of protein powder for an added energy boost.

Vegan S'mores Frappe

- Yield: 1 glass (12 oz / 360 ml)
- Brew Time: ~30 sec (espresso)
- Froth Time: None (blended drink)

Ingredients

- 0.7 oz (20 g) espresso beans (fine grind, double shot)
- 1 cup (240 ml) oat milk
- 1 tbsp chocolate syrup
- ½ cup (120 ml) ice
- Crushed graham crackers and mini marshmallows (for topping)

Instructions

- Brew a **double espresso shot** and let it cool.
- Blend espresso, oat milk, chocolate syrup, and ice until smooth.
- Pour into a tall glass and top with crushed graham crackers and mini marshmallows.

Quick Tip/Variation

- Lightly toast the marshmallows for an extra layer of flavor.

Your Café Note

SYRUPS, TOPPINGS & ADD-ONS

Vanilla Bean Syrup

- Yield: 1 cup (240 ml)
- Brew Time: None (syrup preparation)
- Froth Time: None

Ingredients

- 1 cup (240 ml) water
- 1 cup (200 g) sugar
- 1 vanilla bean, split and scraped (or 2 tsp vanilla extract)

Instructions

- In a saucepan, combine water and sugar over medium heat, stirring until dissolved.
- Add vanilla bean seeds and pod (or vanilla extract) and simmer for 5–10 minutes.
- Remove from heat, discard the pod if used, and cool.
- Store in an airtight container in the fridge for up to 2 weeks.

Quick Tip/Variation

- Use this syrup to sweeten coffee, lattes, or iced drinks for a rich vanilla flavor.

Classic Simple Syrup (Base for All Flavors)

- Yield: 1 cup (240 ml)
- Brew Time: None (syrup preparation)
- Froth Time: None

Ingredients

- 1 cup (240 ml) water
- 1 cup (200 g) sugar

Instructions

- Combine water and sugar in a saucepan over medium heat.
- Stir until the sugar is completely dissolved.
- Remove from heat and let cool.
- Store in an airtight container in the fridge for up to 1 month.

Quick Tip/Variation

- Use this syrup base for flavored syrups (e.g., lavender, ginger) by infusing the syrup with herbs or spices.

Brown Sugar Bourbon Drizzle

- Yield: ½ cup (120 ml)
- Brew Time: None (syrup preparation)
- Froth Time: None

Ingredients

- 1 cup (240 ml) water
- 1 cup (200 g) brown sugar
- 2 tbsp bourbon (optional)

Instructions

- Combine water and brown sugar in a saucepan over medium heat.

- Stir until sugar is dissolved and simmer for 5 minutes.
- Add bourbon and stir until well mixed.
- Remove from heat and let cool.
- Store in an airtight container in the fridge for up to 2 weeks.

Quick Tip/Variation

- Drizzle over lattes, mochas, or desserts for a sweet, caramelized flavor.

Honey Cinnamon Syrup

- Yield: 1 cup (240 ml)
- Brew Time: None (syrup preparation)
- Froth Time: None

Ingredients

- 1 cup (240 ml) water
- 1 cup (200 g) honey
- 1 tsp ground cinnamon

Instructions

- Combine water and honey in a saucepan over medium heat.
- Stir until the honey is fully dissolved.
- Add cinnamon and simmer for 5 minutes.
- Remove from heat and let cool.
- Store in an airtight container in the fridge for up to 2 weeks.

Quick Tip/Variation

- Use in place of sugar syrup for a warm, comforting flavor in fall-inspired drinks.

Maple Pecan Syrup

- Yield: 1 cup (240 ml)
- Brew Time: None (syrup preparation)
- Froth Time: None

Ingredients

- 1 cup (240 ml) water
- 1 cup (200 g) maple syrup
- 2 tbsp pecan syrup or ¼ cup toasted pecans

Instructions

- Combine water and maple syrup in a saucepan over medium heat.
- Stir until the maple syrup is dissolved and simmer for 5–10 minutes.
- Add pecan syrup (or infuse with toasted pecans) and stir well.
- Remove from heat and let cool.
- Store in an airtight container in the fridge for up to 2 weeks.

Quick Tip/Variation

- Drizzle over cold brew, iced lattes, or pancakes for a nutty, maple twist.

Salted Caramel Syrup

- Yield: 1 cup (240 ml)
- Brew Time: None (syrup preparation)
- Froth Time: None

Ingredients

- 1 cup (240 ml) water
- 1 cup (200 g) sugar
- ¼ tsp sea salt
- 1 tsp vanilla extract

Instructions

- Combine water and sugar in a saucepan over medium heat.
- Stir until sugar dissolves, then simmer for 5 minutes.
- Add sea salt and vanilla extract, stirring well.
- Remove from heat and let cool.
- Store in an airtight container in the fridge for up to 2 weeks.

Quick Tip/Variation

- Drizzle over iced lattes or desserts for a sweet-salty kick.

Chocolate Mocha Syrup

- Yield: 1 cup (240 ml)
- Brew Time: None (syrup preparation)
- Froth Time: None

Ingredients

- 1 cup (240 ml) water
- 1 cup (200 g) sugar
- 1 tbsp cocoa powder
- 1 tsp vanilla extract

Instructions

- Combine water and sugar in a saucepan over medium heat.

- Stir until sugar dissolves.
- Whisk in cocoa powder and vanilla extract.
- Simmer for 5–10 minutes, then remove from heat and cool.
- Store in an airtight container in the fridge for up to 2 weeks.

Quick Tip/Variation

- Add a pinch of cinnamon for a spiced mocha twist.

Toasted Coconut Syrup

- Yield: 1 cup (240 ml)
- Brew Time: None (syrup preparation)
- Froth Time: None

Ingredients

- 1 cup (240 ml) water
- 1 cup (200 g) sugar
- ½ cup shredded unsweetened coconut
- 1 tsp vanilla extract

Instructions

- Combine water and sugar in a saucepan over medium heat.
- Stir until sugar dissolves, then simmer for 5 minutes.
- Stir in shredded coconut and vanilla extract.
- Remove from heat, let it steep for 10 minutes, then strain out the coconut.
- Store in an airtight container in the fridge for up to 2 weeks.

- Use toasted coconut flakes for an extra-rich, nutty flavor.

Pumpkin Spice Syrup (Seasonal Favorite)

- Yield: 1 cup (240 ml)
- Brew Time: None (syrup preparation)
- Froth Time: None

Ingredients

- 1 cup (240 ml) water
- 1 cup (200 g) sugar
- 1 tsp pumpkin spice mix
- 1 tbsp pumpkin puree

Instructions

- Combine water and sugar in a saucepan over medium heat.
- Stir until sugar dissolves.
- Add pumpkin spice mix and pumpkin puree, simmering for 5 minutes.
- Remove from heat and let cool.
- Store in an airtight container in the fridge for up to 2 weeks.

Quick Tip/Variation

- Great for adding to lattes, hot chocolate, or iced coffee drinks.

Peppermint Syrup (Holiday Special)

- Yield: 1 cup (240 ml)
- Brew Time: None (syrup preparation)
- Froth Time: None

Ingredients

- 1 cup (240 ml) water
- 1 cup (200 g) sugar
- 1 tbsp peppermint extract
- 1 tsp vanilla extract

Instructions

- Combine water and sugar in a saucepan over medium heat.
- Stir until sugar dissolves and simmer for 5 minutes.
- Remove from heat, stir in peppermint and vanilla extracts.
- Let cool and store in an airtight container in the fridge for up to 2 weeks.

Quick Tip/Variation

- Use this syrup in hot drinks or drizzle over desserts for a festive flavor.

Toasted Marshmallow Foam

- Yield: 1 mug (12 oz / 360 ml)
- Brew Time: None (foam preparation)
- Froth Time: ~45 sec

Ingredients

- ¾ cup (180 ml) milk (dairy or plant-based)
- 2 tbsp marshmallow syrup
- 1 tsp vanilla extract

Instructions

- Froth milk with marshmallow syrup and vanilla extract until thick and foamy.

- Toast marshmallows lightly over a flame (or in the oven) until golden brown.

- Spoon toasted foam on top of your coffee or hot chocolate.

Quick Tip/Variation

- For extra fun, add a toasted mini marshmallow on top as a garnish.

Cold Sweet Cream Foam

- Yield: 1 glass (12 oz / 360 ml)

- Brew Time: None (foam preparation)

- Froth Time: ~30 sec

Ingredients

- ½ cup (120 ml) heavy cream (or coconut cream for dairy-free)

- ½ cup (120 ml) milk (dairy or plant-based)

- 1 tbsp vanilla syrup

Instructions

- Froth cream, milk, and vanilla syrup together until thick and frothy.

- Spoon the foam on top of iced coffee, cold brew, or iced lattes.

Quick Tip/Variation

- Try using caramel syrup for a different flavor twist.

Cinnamon Sugar Dust

- Yield: 1 small jar

- Brew Time: None (dust preparation)

- Froth Time: None

Ingredients

- 2 tbsp ground cinnamon

- 2 tbsp granulated sugar

Instructions

- Mix cinnamon and sugar in a small bowl or jar.

- Sprinkle dust on top of lattes, cappuccinos, or baked goods for a warm, spiced touch.

Quick Tip/Variation

- Use this on churros or donuts for extra flavor.

Espresso Whipped Cream

- Yield: 1 cup (240 ml)

- Brew Time: None (cream preparation)

- Froth Time: ~5 min

Ingredients

- 1 cup (240 ml) heavy cream

- 2 tbsp powdered sugar

- 1 tbsp espresso (cooled)

Instructions

- Whisk heavy cream with powdered sugar and cooled espresso until thick and fluffy.

- Spoon over espresso, lattes, or desserts.

Quick Tip/Variation

- Add a splash of vanilla extract for added depth of flavor.

Cocoa Dusted Almond Topping

- Yield: ~½ cup (120 g)
- Brew Time: None (topping preparation)
- Froth Time: None

Ingredients

- ½ cup (60 g) almonds, chopped
- 1 tbsp cocoa powder
- 1 tbsp powdered sugar

Instructions

- Toast chopped almonds in a dry pan until lightly golden.
- Mix cocoa powder and powdered sugar.
- Sprinkle the cocoa mixture over the toasted almonds.
- Use as a topping for coffee drinks, cakes, or ice cream.

Quick Tip/Variation

- Toss the almonds in a bit of honey before sprinkling cocoa powder for extra sweetness.

Crushed Candy Cane Sprinkles

- Yield: ~½ cup (120 g)
- Brew Time: None (sprinkle preparation)
- Froth Time: None

Ingredients

- 4 candy canes (or peppermint candies)
- 1 tbsp powdered sugar (optional)

Instructions

- Crush candy canes in a plastic bag using a rolling pin until finely ground.
- Mix in powdered sugar for a finer texture (optional).
- Sprinkle over hot or iced lattes, mochas, or holiday drinks.

Quick Tip/Variation

- Store in an airtight container to preserve freshness and avoid moisture.

Hazelnut Praline Drizzle

- Yield: ½ cup (120 ml)
- Brew Time: None (syrup preparation)
- Froth Time: None

Ingredients

- 1 cup (240 ml) water
- 1 cup (200 g) sugar
- 1 tsp hazelnut extract
- 1 tbsp butter (optional, for richness)

Instructions

- Combine water and sugar in a saucepan over medium heat and stir until dissolved.

- Simmer for 5 minutes until syrupy, then stir in hazelnut extract and butter.

- Let cool and drizzle over lattes, mochas, or desserts.

Quick Tip/Variation

- Use as a topping for pancakes or waffles for a café-inspired breakfast.

Spiced Gingerbread Syrup

- Yield: 1 cup (240 ml)

- Brew Time: None (syrup preparation)

- Froth Time: None

Ingredients

- 1 cup (240 ml) water

- 1 cup (200 g) sugar

- 2 tbsp molasses

- 1 tsp ground ginger

- ½ tsp cinnamon

- ¼ tsp cloves

Instructions

- Combine water and sugar in a saucepan over medium heat and stir until dissolved.

- Stir in molasses and spices.

- Simmer for 5–10 minutes, then remove from heat.

- Cool and store in an airtight container.

Quick Tip/Variation

- Use in gingerbread lattes or drizzle over desserts for a holiday twist.

Rose & Cardamom Syrup

- Yield: 1 cup (240 ml)

- Brew Time: None (syrup preparation)

- Froth Time: None

Ingredients

- 1 cup (240 ml) water

- 1 cup (200 g) sugar

- 1 tbsp dried rose petals

- 1 tsp ground cardamom

Instructions

- Combine water and sugar in a saucepan over medium heat.

- Stir until sugar dissolves, then add rose petals and cardamom.

- Simmer for 5 minutes, then strain out rose petals.

- Store in an airtight container.

Quick Tip/Variation

- Use in lattes, teas, or cocktails for a floral, aromatic twist.

Lavender Honey Syrup

- Yield: 1 cup (240 ml)
- Brew Time: None (syrup preparation)
- Froth Time: None

Ingredients

- 1 cup (240 ml) water
- 1 cup (200 g) sugar
- 2 tbsp honey
- 1 tbsp dried lavender flowers

Instructions

- Combine water and sugar in a saucepan over medium heat and stir until dissolved.
- Stir in honey and lavender flowers.
- Simmer for 5 minutes, then strain out lavender.
- Let cool and store in an airtight container.

Quick Tip/Variation

- Use in iced lattes, lemonade, or as a drizzle for desserts.

Your Café Note

CONCLUSION

Building Your Café at Home

Now that you've explored all the recipes and techniques in this book, it's time to bring the café experience into your own home. The Ninja Luxe Café is your perfect partner in creating professional-quality drinks, from rich espressos to frothy lattes, iced coffees, and beyond. With the right tools and techniques, your kitchen will become your personal café, where you can indulge in all your favorite drinks just like a barista would.

How to Keep Experimenting

The fun doesn't stop here! Use the knowledge and recipes you've gained as a springboard to explore even more. Play with different flavors, syrups, and milk alternatives to create your unique drinks. The possibilities are endless, whether it's tweaking a recipe to suit your taste or inventing new combinations, your Ninja Luxe Café is all about creativity. Keep experimenting, and let each cup be an exciting opportunity to try something new!

My words

The most important ingredient in every cup is passion. The Ninja Luxe Café gives you the tools to craft high-quality drinks, but your enthusiasm and willingness to experiment will truly take your creations to the next level. Enjoy every brew, savor the process, and embrace the joy that comes with mastering your favorite café drinks at home.

If you've enjoyed this journey, please consider leaving a review! Your feedback helps me improve and reach more coffee lovers who are eager to create their own café moments.

Printed in Dunstable, United Kingdom